Special Praise for *Life on the Rocks*

"O'Connor is a gifted writer who has a most unique take on addiction and recovery. She makes *Life on the Rocks* accessible and fascinating, using practical insights—not only from the wisdom of philosophers but also from personal experience—to put a new spin on old clichés about what it takes to live a rich, meaningful, and joyful life beyond addiction."

Anne M. Fletcher
Author of *Inside Rehab* and *Sober for Good*

"A wonderful, personal, lyrical book, reflecting on O'Connor's own alcoholism and what it has taught her about honesty, integrity, escapism, self-deception, trauma, and the meaning of life. O'Connor accomplishes the feat of revealing the particulars of her own fascinating life [while creating] a conversation with Socrates, Plato, Aristotle, Kierkegaard, Wittgenstein and others. The book is a down to earth, non-dogmatic meditation on addiction, recovery, and the daunting project of living a good life without numbing one's mind."

Owen Flanagan
James B. Duke Professor of Philosophy
at Duke University

"Peg O'Connor brings her training in philosophy—and her passion for it—to bear on the nature of addiction and, more importantly, recovery from it. Both addicts and philosophers will learn much from her book, as will those who are neither. Her creative use of Nietzsche's notion of the 'Will to Power,' which she distinguishes from 'willpower,' points the way to a life not just lived, but lived well, which she, like Socrates, regards as the universal human goal."

Francis Seeburger
Emeritus Professor of Philosophy at the University of Denver and Author of *Addiction and Responsibility*

"Part philosophical exploration of addiction and recovery, part personal sharing, and part search for suffering's deeper meaning, *Life on the Rocks* is a timely contribution to addiction studies. By emphasizing that addiction not only leads to suffering but is also caused by it, O'Connor reveals just how transformative recovery from addiction truly is."

Dr. Nicholas Plants
Professor of Philosophy at Prince George's Community College and Co-editor of *Sobering Wisdom: Philosophical Explorations of Twelve-Step Spirituality*

"While science, psychology, and sociology have dominated discussion of recovery, philosophy has been largely silent. Now it finally has its say, as O'Connor takes us back to the ancient Greek roots of philosophy as care for the soul. She not only illuminates the recovery process but also shows that philosophy is more than an academic subject—it is a way of life. Life in recovery is a quest for meaning, and philosophy is the ideal guide for the quest."

William Irwin, PhD
Herve A. LeBlanc Distinguished Service Professor of Philosophy at King's College Wilkes-Barre, PA, and Editor of *The Blackwell Philosophy and Pop Culture Series*

"Addiction treatment and academic philosophy are not glamorous fields, but O'Connor puts them together effectively, generating new and fascinating therapeutic tools which address basic questions, such as 'Why live?' O'Connor demonstrates through personal experience and philosophical reasoning how what she teaches in the classroom can help the addict build a positive lifestyle in which psychoactive substances are no longer attractive."

John E. Burns, PhD
Founder of Vila Serena Treatment Centers, Brazil

"Through a series of short reflections that draw upon the work of our great philosophers, *Life on the Rocks* offers helpful, illuminating insights into the experience of addiction and recovery. Peg O'Connor explores the moral import of addiction without ever 'moralizing.' She keeps her thinking close to life and far away from pretension, using accessible language to convey truths that our rationalizations keep hidden from us. She's a philosopher with whom Socrates would have enjoyed conversing."

Jerome A. Miller
Co-editor of *Sobering Wisdom: Philosophical Explorations of Twelve-Step Spirituality*

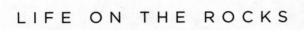

LIFE ON THE ROCKS

PEG O'CONNOR

LIFE
on the ROCKS

FINDING **MEANING**
IN ADDICTION AND RECOVERY

CENTRAL RECOVERY PRESS
LAS VEGAS

Central Recovery Press (CRP) is committed to publishing exceptional materials addressing addiction treatment, recovery, and behavioral healthcare topics.

For more information, visit www.centralrecoverypress.com.

Publisher: Central Recovery Press
3321 N. Buffalo Drive
Las Vegas, NV 89129

21 20 19 18 17 16   1 2 3 4 5

Library of Congress Cataloging-in-Publication Data

Names: O'Connor, Peg, 1965-
Title: Life on the rocks : finding meaning in addiction and recovery / Peg
    O'Connor.
Description: Las Vegas : Central Recovery Press, 2016. | Includes
    bibliographical references.
Identifiers: LCCN 2015036173| ISBN 9781942094029 (pbk.) | ISBN 9781942094036
    (ebook)
Subjects: LCSH: Substance abuse--Patients--Rehabilitation. | Substance
    abuse--Psychological aspects. | Addicts--Behavior modification.
Classification: LCC RC564 .O28 2016 | DDC 362.29--dc23
LC record available at http://lccn.loc.gov/2015036173

Photo of Peg O'Connor by Steven Yang. Used with permission.

Early versions of Chapters Two, Five, and Twenty were first published in the *New York Times* (titled "In the Cave: Philosophy and Addiction," "The Fallacy of the 'Hijacked Brain,'" and "The Light at the End of Suffering," respectively). Reprinted here with permission.

Every attempt has been made to contact copyright holders. If copyright holders have not been properly acknowledged please contact us. Central Recovery Press will be happy to rectify the omission in future printings of this book.

Publisher's Note:
This book contains general information about addiction, addiction recovery, and related matters. The information is not medical advice. This book is not an alternative to medical advice from your doctor or other professional healthcare provider.

Our books represent the experiences and opinions of their authors only. Every effort has been made to ensure that events, institutions, and statistics presented in our books as facts are accurate and up-to-date. To protect their privacy, the names of some of the people, places, and institutions in this book may have been changed.

Cover and interior design and layout by Sara Streifel, Think Creative Design

To my parents, Ann and Jack,
for always giving me your blessing
and support to become whatever
the hell I want to be.

"The greatest hazard of all, losing the self, can occur very quietly in the world, as if it were nothing at all. No other loss can occur so quietly; any loss—an arm, a leg, five dollars, a wife, etc.—is sure to be noticed."

—Søren Kierkegaard, *The Sickness Unto Death*[1]

TABLE OF CONTENTS

ACKNOWLEDGMENTS

THE IMAGE OF AN AUTHOR SCRIBBLING AWAY IN SOLITUDE DOESN'T fit me; writing this book has been a very social and fun enterprise. My friends and family have provided enormous emotional support, intellectual challenge, and gales of laughter. I am evidence of a central theme in this book—the right friends make us better people.

A few friends deserve special mention because I would often bounce ideas off them, and they would happily play along. Mary Beth, Cathy, Sheri, Patty, and Mary are my recovery posse. They would dive into a pig pile to rescue me. In fact, they would do it in great style.

My racquet-wielding friends were especially patient with me when I'd be distracted by a philosophical problem while we were already in the second set. Thanks to VB, Patty, David, Bob, and Will for letting me pound out philosophical confusions on the tennis court even as I swung at volleys. Often after a match, I had an answer to the problem that had distracted me.

I owe my mother more than I could ever calculate, never mind repay. I cherish the conversations we've had while writing this book. The same is true of my brother John, my sister Anne, and my favorite aunt, Lynn. Thanks to Lisa for helping me grow as a philosopher.

Special thanks to philosophy major, Sean Kehren, Gustavus Adolphus College, for his work on the references. Off he marched with the manuscript and a big box of books. Back he came with meticulous endnotes.

Some of the pieces presented here appeared in shorter form on my *Psychology Today* blog, "Philosophy Stirred, Not Shaken," and earlier versions of three chapters were originally published in *The New York Times*. These have been wonderful venues for test-driving my ideas and concepts.

Eliza Tutellier of Central Recovery Press pushed me in all the right ways, which resulted in a much better book. Every writer should have such an editor.

Introduction

PHILOSOPHY AS A
WAY OF LIFE

My name is Peg O'Connor. I am an alcoholic and I am a philosopher. I think many addicts are philosophically inclined and are searching for *a* or *the* meaning of life. We just tend to look in the wrong places for a long time. I know I did. Our lives have provided many opportunities to confront some of the most basic questions about life, which are also some of the most vexing philosophical questions. Addicts live answers to many of these questions. *Life on the Rocks* brings these questions and ways of living into sharper focus, without assuming any familiarity with philosophy.

Addicts struggle with issues of self-identity, moral responsibility, self-knowledge and self-deception, free will and determinism, fatalism, the nature of God, and their relationships with others. These are deeply philosophical concerns, which the natural and social sciences addressing addiction pass right by because they do not lend themselves to empirical investigation. As philosopher Ludwig Wittgenstein (1889–1951) notes, "We feel that even if all possible scientific questions be answered, the problems of life have still not been touched at all."[2] It is a colossal understatement to say that addiction is a huge problem of living.

Addiction can provide an (unwanted) opportunity for a person to confront the most basic existential dilemma: Shall I live or shall I die? Those who choose the former have a Herculean task ahead of them, and ultimately must answer the question, "How *should* I live?" The first philosophers grappled with that question, and we still grapple with it today. We philosophers have a treasure trove of concepts to help people ask and answer that question for themselves. This is the usefulness and value of philosophy. Philosophy can help provide many ways to live these questions and show that there is not only one right way to do so.

I've always said I feel like a throwback in the world of philosophy. My orientation belongs firmly in the ancient world of Greece circa 450 BCE. I turn to the Greeks because they understand philosophy as an activity and as a way of life. Philosophy is an orientation in the world. To be philosophically oriented is to be curious about everything, but especially the nature of the world, the human condition, and an individual's place in the world. Philosophy explores these basic issues, aiming to describe and explain them. Philosophy also aims at prescription, which is most clearly seen in moral philosophy where the most basic concern is how one ought to live. The exploration of any or all these questions is living with a philosophical orientation.

Furthermore, I think of ancient philosophy as the origin of self-help. Socrates, Plato, and Aristotle were concerned with living a good life, which requires a great deal of self-examination. The way to live well is to embody certain character traits and attitudes that lead to self-improvement. Aristotle (384–322 BCE) argued that the happiest life is the virtuous life and only those who have the right sort of concern for their character can realize this. Friends matter importantly to one's character and happiness. Our friends can make us better. The wrong friends can also make us worse off. Any addict would say the same.

The ancients understood the "care of the soul" as the most important undertaking in human life. As the term "soul" may leave some people uncomfortable, I substitute "person" or "self" for "soul." Care of one's self is the most important undertaking in life, and making this claim raises a very important question: Just what is a self?

Consider this question I received from a friend who had been sober for a short while. She asked, "Am I the same person now that I am sober as I was when I was still drinking?" She felt she had a drinking-self and a non-drinking self. Her question grabbed hold of me. I had asked myself a version of this question many times. When I look back on my drinking days—on what I was doing, thinking, and feeling—it now seems as if I am watching someone else's life. In a world of high definition video, I experience my memories like one of those grainy filmstrips popular in the 1960s and 1970s. But those are *my* memories, experiences, and stories. It is *my* life and it is *my* self. In asking the question, "Am I the same person?" I often want the answer to be a resounding "No!" I still feel guilt, shame, embarrassment, and regret at some of the things I remember doing. I do not remember all of it because I was a regular blackout drinker—if I did, it would probably cause me only more grief and shame. While I can imagine some of the things I did, fact tends to be stranger than fiction, so that makes me cringe all the harder. However, I wouldn't be the person I am now, doing the work I am doing, without having had all those experiences. So, in another sense, I do want the answer to be a resounding "Yes, I *am* the same person!"

When my friend asked this question, I was teaching a class in modern (1600–1800) philosophy, and we were reading John Locke's *An Essay Concerning Human Understanding* (1690). One question philosophers were grappling with at the time was, "What unifies a person such that his identity maintains continuity over time?" What ties it all together? One answer Locke offers is memories. Our memories are the ties that bind each of us into a whole.[3] Memories are like the "shrink-wrap" around our consciousness that makes each of us either have or be a continuous self.

I sometimes asked my students, "What about regular blackout drinkers who are still walking, talking, and doing plenty of other things, but have no memory of them? Do such people have a unified self or a divided self? No self? Multiple selves?"

Locke claims that a person's identity doesn't extend to that which he does not remember. The conclusion is that a person who has no memories of his past has no identity. This claim seemed as extreme to my students and my friends as it does to me, in part because even though we may not recall particular incidents, we still believe that they are a part of our identities. We now know that even though few people have conscious memories as toddlers, our experiences at that young age are very much a part of who we are today. We were also uncomfortable with the implications it had for responsibility. If I don't remember doing something, am I not responsible for it? Surely this is not a tenable position.

Having gaping holes in our memories can be very disconcerting; the gaps may be felt acutely. We may spend a huge amount of time trying to fill in the blanks. And where we do not remember, we may be able to imagine. Imagination is a powerful faculty unparalleled in its ability to outstrip other mental faculties. When we act on the basis of imagination, we can find ourselves in all sorts of difficulties in short order.

This discussion about Locke and blackout drinkers is what prompted me to explore addiction and recovery through the lens of Western philosophy. I became convinced that philosophy has a unique contribution to make to our understanding of addiction and recovery and hence the meaning we can make of our lives.

Philosophy may not be the first discipline people would think of as a helpful and friendly companion to understanding addiction and recovery. Some might view it as the last-minute party crasher. Part of the issue is that philosophy has lost its place in our contemporary world: it is both nowhere and everywhere. It is nowhere in the sense that as an academic pursuit philosophy is largely ignored, trivialized, or roundly abused in the larger world. Yet it is everywhere in the sense that philosophy and its perennial questions underpin many of the new academic disciplines.

In a genealogy of academic disciplines (picture a family tree), philosophy has many descendants. In the seventeenth century, "natural philosophy" was an experimental inquiry into the nature of things, which then developed into specific physical sciences such as biology and chemistry. Philosophers were often deeply involved in what we now regularly refer to as scientific inquiry. Philosophers were the original physicians, mathematicians, and even what we now call engineers. René Descartes (1596–1650), known as the Father of Modern Philosophy, invented the Cartesian coordinates (remember the "x" and the "y" axis on which you had to plot points in your high school geometry class?). Another philosopher, Gottfried Wilhelm Leibniz (1646–1716), is arguably the inventor of calculus. William James (1842–1910)—whose work had a profound impact on Bill Wilson and the founding of the fellowship of Alcoholics Anonymous—was an American physician, philosopher, and founder of the American discipline of psychology, which is only about 120 years old. Most recently, neuro- and brain scientists are entering the fray, hypothesizing that addiction is a chronic biochemical condition. But here, too, the questions about the relationship between the mind and the body pop up anew and still resist any obvious answers.

I am not trying to justify philosophy's place in a set of discussions about addiction that has steadily become more scientized and medicalized, but rather I want to show that philosophy underpins many of the questions and methodologies of the different sciences that address addiction. Go far enough and deep enough into any of these disciplines, and you will encounter some of the very philosophical questions that launched their creation. As these new specializations have developed and assert more and more authority in our society, their lineage back to philosophy is more difficult to trace and appreciate. It can seem as if philosophy were regarded as the eccentric elderly relative who gets wheeled out only on special occasions. So I'm wheeling myself out and bringing attention to the experiences that are emblematic of addiction. I'm also exploring the kinds of meanings we are able to make of our addiction and recovery experiences.

Yes, science does rule and has enormous authority in our world. But as Wittgenstein noted, even if all scientific questions are answered, there remain the problems of life. Which brings me back to my colossal understatement: *Addiction is a problem of life.* Rates of addiction have been increasing along with the number of substances and behaviors to which a person can become addicted. With more states legalizing marijuana, the chances of more people becoming addicted increase significantly. If food addiction is legitimized by the American Psychiatric Association, we may see exponential growth in the numbers of people who are addicted. This underscores the need for philosophy to participate in these discussions and for all of us to make use of its rich reserve of concepts and tools that have been sharpened over millennia.

For me, as a philosopher and as an alcoholic, questions about addictions are, at rock bottom, questions about the meaning of life. No discipline frames these sorts of questions as well as philosophy. I am staking a strong claim that philosophy is relevant—perhaps more than ever—in our world and in our lives.

Chapter One

PHILOSOPHICAL DIAGNOSES AND CURES

AN EMBARRASSING ADMISSION IS THAT I NEVER USED TO PAY attention to my alcoholism as part of my identity as a person or as a scholar. It was cordoned off as a fact about me that didn't have a lot of relevance as to who I am or how I am in the world. I certainly never thought it mattered to what I found philosophically compelling. But when I look back on the philosopher who has most influenced me, I've had to shake my head in disbelief that I didn't make more connections sooner. This goes to show the ways a person can be opaque to herself even or especially when she think she knows herself so well.

By training, I am an ethicist and a scholar of Ludwig Wittgenstein, arguably the most important philosopher of the twentieth century. When I first encountered Wittgenstein as an undergraduate student, I was intrigued, dazzled, put off, and utterly stumped. His philosophy was a total puzzle to me, but something in his work and attitude toward philosophy resonated with me. I was bitten by the philosophical bug.

Wittgenstein wrote that working in philosophy is similar to working in architecture. It is more of a "working on oneself" in which a person has his own interpretation, way of seeing things, and expectations.[4] The reference to architecture may sound odd, but Wittgenstein believed good architecture had to embody certain virtues or traits that were also important for being a good person and living a good life. Wittgenstein regarded himself as an architect. In conjunction with an actual trained architect, Wittgenstein designed a house for one of his sisters in Vienna in 1925. Architecture must demonstrate good proportion, balance, simplicity, functionality, and congruity both within a building and between the building and its environment. Proportion and balance are related; a large room with small windows strikes a discordant chord. Something feels off when you enter a room where the windows are not in proportion to the size of the room and do not align with one another. Simplicity is pleasing. Wittgenstein had no tolerance for design elements that had no function and served no real purpose. They are distracting ornamentations. Congruity relates to the entire property: Is the house in agreement with its environment? A Swiss Chalet in the midst of an urban setting would seem out of place, wrong even. There is a beauty to congruity and an ugliness or failure to incongruity.

Philosophy, like architecture, embodies these same elements or virtues. Philosophy should aim to help a person realize balance, simplicity, proportion, and functionality so that she can design a life that has congruity. One's life—one's house—can be congruent with the world around oneself.

A philosopher's work, according to Wittgenstein, is to liberate herself and others from bewitching pictures, skewed conceptual schemes, and unreasonable and perhaps unjustified expectations. The practice of philosophy is a remedy for confusion that disrupts the balance or congruity of one's beliefs and actions. Whether the confusion is induced by the outside world or self-inflicted, it makes it more difficult to stay connected to and in agreement with the world. In other words, Wittgenstein was trying to get rid of the "stinkin' thinkin'" of philosophers. That is a huge task, as he kept realizing. Above all else, philosophy ought to aim for clarification— of oneself, one's place in the world, and the ways one derives meaning from life. Philosophy, when practiced well, can be useful. It can enable us to grapple in productive ways with questions about the meaning of life and who *I* am and how *I* want to be in the world.

For Wittgenstein, as well as for Socrates, Plato, and Aristotle, philosophy has a built-in moral command to become a better person. Anyone who is trying to live a life of recovery is trying to become a better person, which is why philosophy, addiction, and recovery belong together.

Using illness and disease metaphors, Wittgenstein talks about philosophy, culture, or our times. Philosophy as typically practiced generates as much confusion as it does clarification, which explains why Wittgenstein spent so much time diagnosing the "sicknesses" of philosophy. He believed that much of what philosophers did created false problems, which they then spent (wasted) a great amount of time and energy trying to solve. This tendency might sound familiar to addicts.

Wittgenstein takes a striking approach to philosophical problems: rather than solve them, he believed one ought to dissolve them. Many of the problems that have vexed philosophers for centuries are pseudo-problems that arise from our having certain expectations, assumptions, and beliefs about how things should be. For example, many people believe they are completely transparent to themselves but entirely opaque to all others, as if each of us were a self-contained privacy unit. This makes it difficult, if not impossible, to understand others, because each of us can only understand herself. We become bewitched by this picture of human nature and interaction. Wittgenstein's aim is to help us shake off this bewitchment, so that we may see/experience/inhabit the world differently. When we can do that, we can make different meanings, bringing us back to the meaning-of-life questions. It is along these lines that Wittgenstein's philosophy and amplifications of it have much to offer discussions about addiction and recovery.

A person's history and experiences are important in understanding her philosophy. Learning about Wittgenstein's life made me see him as a fellow traveler, one who appears never to have been comfortable in his own skin. As a person, he makes a kind of sense to me, even though our life stories are radically different. Learning about him as a person also has helped me understand why he was concerned with particular questions and why he found so many "answers" unsatisfactory.

Wittgenstein was a tortured man, for all kinds of good reasons. Born to enormous wealth in Vienna in 1889, his formidable family provided the type of fodder that could keep a stable of phychoanalysts happy for many careers. Wittgenstein had a father who was an overbearing captain of industry, at least two older brothers who committed suicide, a third brother who died when he seemed to intentionally put himself in harm's way, and another brother, Paul, who was a concert pianist who lost his right arm in World War I, as well as doting and commanding older sisters. He gave away his portion of his family wealth to his relatives in the belief that, since they were already so rich, more money couldn't possibly corrupt them. He lived in England for most of his adult life except for a brief period in Norway, where he was a notoriously unsuccessful elementary school teacher. His family was Jewish and during World War II, his sisters made a deal with the Nazi regime that allowed them to continue to live in Vienna in exchange for their gold and other holdings. This so offended and affected their brother Paul that he never spoke to them again.

No matter his age or accomplishments, Wittgenstein viewed anything less than total genius as abject failure. His thoughts about himself and his place in the world were black and white; everything for him was all-or-nothing. Talk about high expectations breeding low self-esteem. Sound familiar? The man was tortured, and philosophy was for him both the illness and the cure. It had a hold on him.[5]

Wittgenstein's odd and tortured ways of being in the world show up in his philosophy, especially when he is trying to identify all that we take for granted in our own worldviews and how we typically project our assumptions about the way things should be onto other people and different ways of living. This was another aspect of his work that simultaneously attracted and repelled me. His examples often take readers aback. For example, he asks: What would you do if you encountered a person selling wood who priced by height rather than volume? At first, you'd think it makes no sense; it seems stupid or wrong or the person must have fallen off the turnip truck back at the bend. But Wittgenstein challenges us to excavate those assumptions and to explore where the lines are between sense and nonsense and what the limitations and difficulties are in trying to understand people who, in effect, operate with some really different organizing principles.

What are we willing to let go of, and what will we hold onto, regardless of how many of our other beliefs we must sacrifice? To people who are not addicted, addicts seem to operate with as skewed a worldview as those wood sellers. What kind of people would risk their livelihoods when the boss has threatened to fire them for being too hungover to work? Who would forsake their family and give up their dreams just to get high? It seems crazy that people do these things, but it seems just as crazy that other nonaddicted people get sucked into our worlds, believing they may be able to make a person stop using. These really are meaning-of-life questions and have a familiar ring to addicts.

Introducing Wittgenstein and his approach to philosophy serves to explain my approach in this book. Like Wittgenstein and the ancients, I believe there is no higher obligation than caring for your soul or your self, and philosophy is an important means to that end. Philosophy aims to make its practitioners better people. When we don't care for our person in all its dimensions—mental, physical, emotional, social, and spiritual—we run the risk of creating a great deal of confusion and suffering. In our addictions we create confusion and suffering for ourselves and for those around us. By not caring for our person, we are not capable of the best sort of life, as Aristotle would say.

Like Wittgenstein, I understand diagnosis to be an important function of philosophy. Using some of the central concepts of philosophy, I describe and diagnose some of those "problems of life" emblematic of addiction. Good diagnosis always aims to identify the source of the problem so that one treats the cause and not just the symptoms. The symptoms matter enormously, and a person can experience great relief when they are treated. But if the underlying cause is not adequately addressed, recurrence is a likely outcome.

The work of Søren Kierkegaard (1813–1855) is also important to this task. Kierkegaard stands out from other philosophers in his ability to explore what each person is up against in herself (one of the reasons Wittgenstein was so taken by Kierkegaard's work). Kierkegaard shows us how we can hinder and even lose ourselves in all sorts of ways: One of the most surprising ways is that we can lose ourselves and be in great despair when we are happy. As Kierkegaard says, "deep, deep within the most secret hiding place of happiness there dwells anxiety . . . for despair the most cherished and desirable place to live is in the heart of happiness."[6]

My work follows Wittgenstein's methodology, and my aim in this book is to diagnose by describing some of the forms of suffering that accompany addiction. As mentioned previously, addicts often suffer from self-deception, which has many faces or guises. Rationalization, denial, and minimization are some of the more familiar forms. At first glance, other forms are less familiar, but just as common and dangerous, including shame, lack of self-trust, hedging your bets, procrastination, and feeling like a moral failure by placing demands on yourself that cannot possibly be met.

As Wittgenstein notes, the "cure" involves changing how one sees and understands a problem or situation. Diagnosis alone is not sufficient; however, it is an important step to the dissolution of problems. Understanding without action is purely ornamental; action dissolves problems. For example, a person who always worried about being caught in lies about his using *dissolves* that worry when he stops using. That worry is no longer viable because his actions are different. One important action that must be taken repeatedly is making a passionate commitment to different ways of living. Such a commitment may lead to what Aristotle calls "flourishing" and many others might call a life of great recovery.

Chapter Two

HOW IS ADDICTION LIKE
LIVING IN A CAVE?

PHILOSOPHY HAS ALWAYS BEEN ABOUT THE PURSUIT OF KNOWLEDGE, BUT one with the higher or loftier goal of living a good and just life. This pursuit has involved examining the nature of just about everything. Socrates, one of the first Greek philosophers, who appears as a character in the Dialogues of Plato (his student), always asked a guiding question, "What is it?" The "it" could be justice, piety, beauty, courage, temperance, or knowledge. For Socrates, these are the crucial virtues around which life should revolve, which is why he interrogated people when they invoked these concepts. His agenda was to draw the line between what appears to be just or pious, for example, and what justice or piety really are. The stakes are enormously high; Socrates once engaged a man who was prosecuting his own father for impiety or offense to the gods. Socrates attempted (unsuccessfully) to get this man to see that prosecuting his own father might be the impious act.

In his pursuit of knowledge about the nature of virtues, Socrates first had to debunk popular opinions about them. Popular opinion tends to have a stronghold on many of us. Debunking happened in the context of a dialogue, but in reality, it more closely resembled a cross-examination. Socrates looked for the essence, the "necessary property," or "ineliminable trait" that made particular acts pious or just. He interrogated every definition offered to him by asking for examples, pushing and pulling against those definitions, turning them inside out and upside down, stretching that definition to see if weird things followed, exploring what follows when a particular definition is put into practice, and excavating hidden assumptions in those definitions. Being in a dialogue with Socrates was intellectual gymnastics on an Olympic level, and for good reason: Socrates took his philosophizing as a commitment to help people avoid making mistakes that would have long-lasting if not eternal effects on their soul. This isn't exactly glamorous work, but it is vital in the pursuit of knowledge of any sort. Socrates' work prompted the seventeenth century philosopher John Locke (1632–1704) to describe himself as an under-laborer, clearing away the rubbish that gets in the way of acquiring knowledge.[7] We now call this work conceptual analysis, one of the most powerful tools a philosopher has to wield.

How does philosophy approach or provide us with a better understanding of addiction? How can we engage with popular views about it? Socrates would ask, "What is it?" And he wouldn't be alone: psychiatrists, psychologists, chemical dependency counselors, and people in recovery programs are asking this question. Neuroscientists have entered the fray, searching for both the cause and effective management of addiction. Yet there is no definitive consensus on what addiction is or on what substances and behaviors have the potential to become addictive. Defining addiction remains an area of heated debate, with incredibly huge stakes on both a personal level and on social and public policy levels.

Despite differences of opinion, most of us can recognize—and through recognition, perhaps better understand—certain behaviors and situations in which "normal" use of alcohol and other drugs turns to destructive dependency. We can see a problem even if we cannot agree on an exact definition or description of it.

One sort of recognition can be found in examining allegory, in this case a very familiar one from Plato. Allegory—a story that functions as an extended metaphor that has both literal and figurative meanings—is clearly not science. It won't offer an explanation of addiction, but it does offer the potential for a sort of insight that conceptual analysis cannot. An allegory allows us to unpack many of those dimensions that escape more scientific description. With the cave allegory Plato uses in the *Republic* to draw the line between appearance and reality, we have a powerful tool for understanding the crisis of the addicted person.

In the allegory, Plato tells about a group of prisioners who are inside a cave chained facing a wall. They cannot move their heads and, therefore, cannot look sideways or behind; they can only look forward. Behind them is a burning fire and a half wall where puppeteers hold up puppets that cast shadows. To the chained men, the shadows are real; they have no concept of the real objects that are causing the shadows. They mistake appearance for reality, and thus they have no knowledge.

Now imagine that the prisoners are released from their chains. They look behind them and see the objects that caused the shadows. Most likely they will be confused and unwilling to accept that these objects caused the shadows. Imagine now that the prisoners start to leave the cave. They will be painfully blinded as soon as they encounter daylight. Once their eyes adjust, they will be confronted by a harsh, bright world with a whole host of horrifying objects.

Some of the prisoners will flee back to the safety of the darkness and shadows, valuing the familiar more than the unfamiliar. Anyone who returns to tell his friends who are still enchained what he has seen will be regarded as a crazy person lacking any credibility. Others, once their eyes have more fully adjusted to the light, will want to stay above ground. Such people come to realize that the world of light is the real one where genuine knowledge is possible. Certain people among those who have "seen the light" of truth and reality will feel compelled to go back into the cave to help those who are still enchained to leave the cave. This is the philosopher's burden, according to Plato.[8]

This allegory is richly wonderful for understanding addiction, relapse, and recovery. Most people who become addicted become enchained to their drug of choice. The word "addiction" comes from the Latin verb "addicere," which means to give over, dedicate, or surrender. In the case of many alcoholics, for instance, including my own, this is just what happens. What may have started as fun and harmless use begins to grow troubling, painful, and difficult to stop. The alcoholic becomes chained to alcohol in a way that is different from others who "drink normally."

In various scenarios of addiction, the addicted person's fixation on a shadow reality—one that does not conform to the world outside his or her use—is apparent to others often well before it is apparent to the addict. When the personal cost of using becomes noticeable, it can still be written off or excused as merely atypical. Addicts tend to orient their activities around their addictive behavior; they may forego friends and activities where using is not featured. Some isolate themselves; others change their circle of friends in order to be with people who use in the same way they do or worse than they do so that they can appear "normal" or "not as bad." They engage in faulty, yet persuasive, addicted reasoning, willing to use anything as evidence that they do not have a problem; no amount of reasoning will persuade them otherwise. Each time the addict makes a promise to cut down or stop, but does not, the chains get more constricting. Each time she does something she promised herself she would never do again, the chains become tighter still.

Yet, for many reasons, some people begin to wriggle against the chains of addiction. Whether it is an experience that scares them to death (not uncommon), or losing something that really matters (also not uncommon), or looking in the mirror and not recognizing themselves or not liking what they see (quite common), some people begin to work themselves out of the chains. People whose descent into addiction came later in life have more memories of what life can be like not using. Some will be able to turn and see the fire and the half wall and recognize the puppets causing the shadows. Those whose use started so young that it is all they really know will often experience the fear and confusion Plato described. But, as sometimes happens in recovery, they can start to come out of the cave, too. And, often, they are guided by another who made it.

The brightness of the light can be painful, as many addicts realize once their use stops. The pain from physical withdrawal can be excruciating. People fear pain, and that fear can enchain a person, too. There's also a kind of emotional withdrawal. Substances and addictive behaviors provide the possibility of relief from pain and suffering. This possibility sustains us until we can use. The difficulty of emotional withdrawal shouldn't be underestimated. Many people fear facing an emotional tsunami. Those who used to numb feelings or avoid painful memories may feel defenseless. Often we lack the tools and skills to name our emotions; our emotional palates are usually limited. This is why some, even many, will retreat back to the familiar darkness of the cave. Too much is new and scary; they may feel and be ill-equipped to lead their lives in different ways. Back with using friends, they will find comfort, or what we understand as relapse.

Some will make it farther out of the cave and allow their eyes to adjust. They may struggle to stay in recovery and remain balanced. So many of their old coping behaviors will not work, and they will be faced with a seemingly endless task of learning how to rebuild their emotional lives. Some will achieve and live in recovery for a good while and later relapse. People relapse for all sorts of reasons. Often these have to do with old ways of thinking and behaving that may begin with a foray into one area of life that at some point becomes a roaring comeback in other areas of life. When people who have had some recovery relapse and go back to the darkness of the cave, they may be met with derision—an "I told you so" attitude. But at least they are returning to something familiar and can tell themselves, "I tried but couldn't do it." This may serve as justification for not trying again for a long time, if ever again.

Those who do make it out of the cave and manage not to relapse are few and far between. They know how precarious their recovery is and what they need to do to maintain it. People in long-term recovery are often the ones who need to go back into the cave, not as saviors, but for their own survival. People with years of recovery often say that newcomers help them stay sober because their pain, loss, and confusion are so fresh. Their stories remind old-timers of life enchained in the cave. Old-timers can share their stories, too, and in the process show newcomers different ways to be in the world.

Of course our stories are real and deeply personal, but, siminlar to allegories, they can wield a transformative power. Hearing shared refrains of their own experiences in stories and allegories provides people with an important corrective lens. It leads some to see and understand themselves and the world differently. Equipped with this knowledge, people can begin to transform their lives.

Chapter Three

EXISTENTIAL CONCUSSIONS

SUFFERING IS A PART OF LIFE. WHETHER BROUGHT ON BY the "slings and arrows of outrageous fortune," as William Shakespeare's Hamlet ponders, by our own actions or those of others, or by unpredictable natural or man-made disasters, suffering happens.[9] Humans are resilient and able to tolerate all sorts of suffering. And many do believe, along with Friedrich Nietzsche, that what doesn't kill us only makes us stronger.

Many of the classics in Western literature are tales of meaningful suffering. We devour these stories because we love how people are able not only to make sense of their suffering but also transform it so that it serves a higher purpose. A perfect example is Sydney Carton in Charles Dickens's classic, *A Tale of Two Cities*. Set in France at the time of the French Revolution, Sydney Carton is an unexceptional, possibly alcoholic, young attorney who lacks any confidence or purpose in his life. Carton does bear an uncanny resemblance to a French aristocrat, Charles Darnay, who has been sentenced to death at the guillotine. Carton loves Darnay's wife, Lucie. Out of this love, Carton tricks Darnay and trades places with him so that he may be executed. It isn't until he sacrifices himself for love that he finds meaning and peace. His last words are some of the most famous in English literature. He says, "It is a far, far better thing that I do, than I have ever done; it is a far, far better rest I go to than I have ever known."[10]

As noble as it may be to make huge sacrifices for others or to dedicate one's life to a higher calling or purpose, there are times when it is simply not possible. Life presents many instances when a person cannot make sense of her suffering. This is the kind of suffering Nietzsche identifies as intolerable and life destroying. In the throes of this sort of suffering, a person experiences an existential concussion.

A concussion is a brain injury that results from a blow to the head or violent shaking. The brain is either shaken or moves back and forth within the skull. A concussion alters the brain's function for a period of time that is directly related to the severity of the concussion. By analogy, an existential concussion is caused by a sharp blow or a violent shaking of a person's life conditions—such as a sudden death, traumatic injury, or end of a long-term relationship. An existential concussion is both a cause and a consequence of acute suffering that is characterized by a lack of meaning.

These concussions have degrees of severity and some combination of the following manifestations is common: compromised decision-making ability; significant impairment in perspective such that one is not able to inhabit alternate viewpoints; disorientation in the world such that one does not know who one is, where one belongs, or how one fits in the world; difficulty in transforming one's suffering into something meaningful; despair that one has no freedoms and no possibilities; absence of meaning and value in one's own life that expands to nihilism about there being any meaning and value in the world; and loss or destruction of the primary framework in which a person orients her life.

Existential concussions can occur in a variety of ways, but all of them involve a separation from the primary framework that has provided a person with adequate conditions for making sense of *all* her experiences, including suffering. Consider a person of faith who suffers a series of tragedies. She may wonder if she has done something to deserve this. She might also start to wonder about a God she's always understood to be loving and kind allowing such suffering. Or, even more upsetting to her, she may wonder how God could inflict such suffering.

Her faith had been the axis around which her life revolved to explain both good fortune and loss. Having that axis tilt might cause a mild to moderate concussion. Having that axis ripped out suddenly would cause a severe existential concussion. Knock out the axis and everything it held in place will fall. When this occurs, the framework of her faith no longer provides viable conditions for making sense of what has happened. Nothing in her faith provides an explanation or amelioration, and so the sufferer may reject all or part of the framework. She may reject it in defiance with a mighty scream, or she may reject it with a quiet whimper. If enough time passes, the person who has lost her faith may become incomprehensible to herself and to those with whom she shared a faith. She is alienated from herself and others, which only exacerbates the effects of an existential concussion. This alienation may fuel behavior that becomes addictive.

Addictions are themselves causes and consequences of existential concussions. As an addiction progresses, a person often begins to trade away—even in small amounts—some of the commitments and principles that have been crucial to his sense of self. The addict may slowly start to do things he promised he would never do. He may start to lower his standards for his own "acceptable behavior." Trade away too many of these commitments and a person may no longer recognize himself. He may look in the mirror and see a stranger. This disorientation may become full-blown alienation, which in turn may fuel addictive behaviors that further fuel alienation.

The addiction/existential concussion of one person may also contribute to the existential concussion of others. Many existential concussions involve what psychologist Pauline Boss calls "ambiguous loss."[11] Boss offers two categories of ambiguous loss. The first is when a person is physically absent but psychologically present, such as a soldier missing in action and presumed dead or a child who has been kidnapped. An active addict who abandons his family may also fall into this category. He's both there and not there, which affects the family dynamic in uncountable ways. Hoping and wishing for someone's return or remaining furious about someone's abandonment may become an axis around which other concerns of the family revolve.

The second type of ambiguous loss is when a person is physically present but psychologically absent, such as a person with dementia or someone suffering from significant mental illness. An active addict parent who attends primarily to his use may fall into this category. He's both there and *not* there. His presence and his moods define the dynamics of his family. Everyone in the family may try to act in ways that do not draw his attention or upset him in any way. Walking on eggshells becomes the family pattern.

Ambiguous losses do not fit easily into our patterns of grief and loss. A person is either present or absent, alive or dead. One is either single, married/partnered, divorced, or widowed. Dichotomous categories are always the most rigid. Each time a person hits the rigid limits of these categories or careens back and forth between them, she may become a little more disoriented and full of more despair. Disorientation and despair cause more careening and a vicious cycle begins.

Consider the varying ways that different illnesses and the suffering of individuals and their families are regarded. In a poignant article, "Food Comfort," Larry M. Lake describes a "tsunami of food offerings [as] an edible symbol of our community's abundant generosity," when his wife is diagnosed with breast cancer.[12] The outpouring of concern took many forms—rides to appointments, notes and cards, and telephone calls. As crass as it sounds, his wife had the "right" sort of illness, one that people acknowledge. The family's suffering was recognized and shared, which contributes to it being meaningful.

There is no such acknowledgment ten years later when Lake's daughter is admitted to a psychiatric hospital with bipolar disorder following years of alcohol and drug abuse. Clearly his daughter is ill, but it isn't the sort of illness that elicits a community's acknowledgment. No one brings you dinner when your daughter is an addict.

A person can also experience ambiguous loss of her own person. This can be one of the most profound forms of alienation. Consider the ways that a person often recognizes—even at the same time as she denies—how she is losing parts of herself to her addiction. Commitments, values, activities, and dreams that once made her feel alive, valuable, connected, and like she was contributing to the world, start to fall by the wayside. She is still physically present, but pieces of her are now missing.

When she is no longer capable of caring for her person or has no interest in doing so, she is psychologically absent in significant ways. Addiction causes a person to lose parts of herself when she loses important relationships that have become fundamentally fused into her identity and her self-understanding. She may no longer be someone's partner. She is no longer the best friend. She is no longer the parent who is actively engaged in her child's life. Without these relationships that have been so life affirming, she is not able to care for her person. This is ambiguous loss.

The ambiguous loss of a person to herself does not fit neatly into our more usual and recognized categories of loss. People whose experiences of loss fall into the cracks and fissures of frameworks keep hitting jagged edges. No wonder they are concussed and find themselves on a precipice.

Are there ways to prevent existential concussions? Not even the best-padded helmet is sufficient to prevent all concussions. But we can effect changes in the conditions that contribute to existential concussions and make them less likely and less severe. One way to do this is to continue to expand our understanding and acknowledgment of types of suffering, especially those that relate to ambiguous loss. We can also work against the stigmatization of groups of people, which has happened with many types of addiction.

Recovery from addiction involves making or finding meaning that begins to orient a person in her life and the broader world. Some people will do well in a program that provides an easily recognizable framework, such as a twelve-step fellowship. Some desire different frameworks that make no reference to powerlessness or a higher power; they may incline to something more secular. Yet others will want a more explicitly faith-based model or a more therapeutic model. Some will eschew ready-made frameworks in favor of ones that are more of their own construction.

Regardless of the particular framework, people begin to orient their actions and their lives around recovery. Recovery becomes an axis around which life can turn. Recovery is a passionate commitment to living a life of self-care, self-examination, and respectful connection to others.

Chapter Four

FROM WILLPOWER TO
WILL TO POWER

WILLPOWER IS A POPULAR SUBJECT THESE DAYS. CHANNEL YOUR WILLPOWER in all the right ways, and you can transform your life. Or so it seems. In an interesting and provocative book, *Willpower: Rediscovering the Greatest Human Strength*, Roy Baumeister and John Tierney argue that willpower has a physical basis and functions like a muscle. Willpower can be strengthened, and it can be depleted. It is a finite resource, so one ought to expend it wisely. Glucose puts the power in willpower; when levels of glucose are low, willpower diminishes. Raise glucose levels, and willpower increases, too.[13]

It all seems so straightforward. If a person puts herself on the right regimen, she can build her willpower muscles so that she is totally ripped. Then she'll be able to do anything because her reserves will be plentiful. If, along the way, she becomes savvier about where and when she expends her willpower, there is a compounding effect on her reserves.

This view of willpower raises interesting questions for addiction. Are some addictive behaviors beyond the control of willpower? Many experts in the field of addiction studies would say a full-blown or extreme addiction is beyond the pull of willpower, and the diagnosis of substance use disorder in the DSM-5 now involves a spectrum from mild to moderate use to extreme use.[14]

Some of the old questions about willpower will return, especially for those who are closer to the mild and slightly moderate end of the spectrum and who could pivot back toward "normal" use or abstinence. Are these "mild" addicts simply not directing their willpower in the proper way if they progress down the spectrum? Or are they not properly "willpower working out" so that they are not building strong temptation-resisting muscles while they still can? These questions raise the specter of the old familiar view that addicts are moral failures because we lack self-control to stop our destructive behaviors. We're either impetuous and act without thinking or we know what we should do but still give in to the temptation. Either way, it will be crucial to break the link between willpower and moral failure. This is one link in a chain of reasoning that, when internalized by people struggling with addiction, may contribute to a fatalistic attitude. Why bother to stop when someone *like me* can never change?

Willpower is equated with self-control and saying no. The idea is that we exert willpower when we resist temptation. The temptation can be of any sort—that delicious piece of cake, the extra twenty minutes napping on the couch, surfing the web while at work, or the twelve pack of beer in the refrigerator—and willpower is the ability to say no. Part of the problem is that the same reserve of willpower has to resist all temptations; there aren't pools of willpower for *this* sort of temptation and other pools for *that* sort of temptation.

Willpower also plays a positive role and helps us achieve goals that we have decided are important to us. Willpower motivates us to stick with positive resolutions. But even here, there is still a strong negative function. My healthy eating now means that I need to say no to the chocolate-glazed doughnut taunting me from the bakery case.

Saying no to things is exhausting, as Baumeister and Tierney argue. We live in a world of unending temptations, and it can seem as if we are constantly caught in a deluge of wants and desires. Having said no to ninety-nine things makes it more likely that we cannot resist when the hundredth temptation crosses our path.

So, all those times we resist what are weaker temptations for us while thinking, *Oh, now I am really building those willpower muscles*, we may actually be setting ourselves up for even greater failures. Many addicts I know who were the "use because I've been working so hard" variety are perhaps especially vulnerable to this dynamic. When that hundredth temptation overcomes us, what we may see is total defeat. Many addicts tend to be black or white and all-or-nothing thinkers. We live life trying to jump across a vast space that allows for no middle ground.

Even though giving into the temptation may at first feel like a defeat, it also provides something of a relief. We seem to believe that if we cannot say no 100 percent of the time, we might as well never say no. Our failure serves as justification for never trying again. Furthermore, we might begin to think that a lack of self-control in one area of our life is proof that we just lack all self-control. Since we are constitutionally incapable of self-control, why bother to try to exercise control in other areas of our lives? This way of thinking is familiar to many addicted people and breeds a sort of fatalism.

There is an implicit formula undergirding this concept of willpower in conjunction with addiction that reads "inability to resist temptation = addiction." All parts of the formula—inability, resistance, temptation, and addiction—are worrisome. It would seem to follow that the further a person moves down the substance use disorder continuum (mild to severe), the less she is able to exert self-control to resist the temptation of her drug of choice. A person either loses the ability she once had to resist or develops the inability as she moves along the continuum. But what space is there to explore the conditions under which she loses the ability completely? Does aging affect our ability to resist? How does familial or social support affect ability? These sorts of questions fall off the table. Instead the focus remains on the individual and her failure to exert her self-control in the right direction to the right degree.

To understand the connection between having power and having the opportunity to exercise it, consider this analogy: In the United States, citizens aged eighteen and older have the right to vote (unless it has been revoked due to conviction of certain crimes). But there are all sorts of conditions that keep people from exercising it, some of which are beyond a person's control. Public transportation may not be easily available or available at all. Even though employees are entitled to exercise their right to vote during the workday, some may not do so out of fear of negative consequence from their bosses.

Willpower may be difficult to build if people live in conditions that pose very real and significant temptations or challenges. A common example is people newly in recovery who continue to live with their using friends or family. Leaving the situation may not be a realistic option. While it is true that they do have *some* power to make choices, those choices are largely shaped by considerations that are well beyond their control.

What does it mean to resist a substance or behavior that is tempting? It might seem obvious that it requires not consuming certain substances or abstaining from an activity such as gambling. The spectrum of use disorder may require a recalibration of the concepts of resistance and abstinence. Resistance may include harm reduction or moderate use when it's not accompanied by the sort of negative consequences that follow from more disordered use. Abstinence, too, may stand in need of newer understandings, which is most clearly seen in the case of food addiction. One cannot completely abstain from food. Is not consuming particular foods or not consuming to specified quantities abstinence? It certainly seems like a form of resistance. Also, what if a person still orients her life around that substance or behavior or keeps many of the same "using" behaviors in the absence of the substance? There is resistance to the behavior but does there also need to be resistance to the thinking?

A deeper worry is the assumption that temptations are easily identified and defined. The nature and quality varies greatly between different sorts of temptations. On the one hand, a temptation is a temptation is a temptation. All temptations are on par with one another. On the other hand, though, each of us has multiple temptations, some of which are much stronger than others. Is anything tempting potentially addictive? All temptations are not created equal. Some substances are manufactured to be irresistible temptations (potato chips, anyone?).

The formula "inability to resist temptation = addiction" reduces a complex set of phenomena to one characteristic: the failure of an individual to exert the right amount of self-control in the right direction. But how do we determine the "right" amount and the "right" direction? Consider people with cross-addictions. A person who is trying to quit drinking may decide not to quit smoking at the same time. Co-occurring mental health concerns complicate the picture even further.

A final concern is that conjoining willpower and addiction produces a companion formula, which would state that "ability to resist temptation = recovery." For some people, abstinence may be a necessary condition for recovery, but by itself it isn't sufficient. Willpower is primarily a negative force; it is about saying no to things. People who are governed by willpower become masters of denying themselves, such that it becomes the dominant way to treat everything that comes their way.

Nietzsche might argue that willpower is a means by which people wedge themselves into acceptability and respectability by denying parts of themselves or what they really value. So many of us try to wedge ourselves into "acceptability" and "respectability" in order to avoid the judgment of others and ourselves. We internalize judgments and standards and then judge ourselves and others for thinking, feeling, living, and loving the way we may really want. We lose our individuality and vitality, Nietzsche would say, when we subscribe to these negative judgments. Part of the rub is that even if we feel torn or a deep sense of unease about these values we are trying so hard to fulfill, we still will feel like a failure when we cannot embody them well. We are more likely to think there is something wrong with us than to think there is something wrong with a system of values and beliefs that we cannot possibly live up to. It would never occur to us to reject those individual values or the broader moral system in which those values have their homes. This may be the situation of a religiously conservative person who believes that homosexuality is a sin. If she begins to tentatively question her own sexuality, just about everything in her belief system will say it is sinful and wrong. The first stop in her thinking will inevitably be "there's something wrong with me," rather than, "my belief system may be wrong about this."

If we are successful in embodying values with which we feel such a lack of ease and wedge ourselves into ways of living that cause us angst and anxiety, we risk losing important pieces of ourselves. This makes it very hard if not impossible to lead a fulfilling life or to live a happy life in recovery.

How is it possible to lead a fulfilling and happy life when saying no is your default? We need something that pushes us to say yes to some things in life, perhaps to our entire life. It may require what Nietzsche describes as "will to power."[15]

Will to power is a positive force. It motivates or drives people to live in ways that lead to self-fulfillment and flourishing. Will to power is having the courage to face yourself for who you really are, as opposed to what you appear to be to others or what others believe you should be. Embodying will to power is having the strength and conviction to live your life actively embracing values that you have chosen. This is the opposite of living a life based on values that you have passively and unquestioningly taken on.

Saying yes to your life is a heroic undertaking; it is grabbing hold of life. A person may feel as if she has to jump out of the familiar and comfortable. A person living her life on her terms is the exception. Living in recovery is a manifestation of will to power. A person's decision to change her use of certain drugs or behaviors requires bravery. In choosing recovery, a person says much more than no to certain substances or behaviors. She is saying yes to herself and taking responsibility for what she has done, who she is now, and what she hopes to be in the future.

Chapter Five

DOES ADDICTION
HIJACK THE BRAIN?

OF ALL THE PHILOSOPHICAL DISCUSSIONS THAT SURFACE IN CONTEMPORARY LIFE, the question of free will—mainly the debate over whether or not we have it—is certainly one of the most persistent. That might seem odd, as the average person rarely seems to pause to reflect on whether his or her choices on, say, where to live, whom to marry, or what to eat for dinner are his or her own or the inevitable outcome of a deterministic universe. Still, the spate of "can't help yourself" books would indicate that people are in fact deeply concerned with how much of their lives they can control. Perhaps that's because, upon further reflection, we find that our understanding of free will lurks beneath many essential aspects of our existence.

One particularly interesting variation on this question appears in scientific, academic, and therapeutic discussions about addiction. Many times, the question is framed as follows: "Is addiction a disease or a choice?" The issue of willpower lurks in the framing of this question. Something that is chosen is assumed to be subject to willpower and hence a matter of personal responsibility. Willpower assumes that we have free will. What rides on the answer is the degree to which an individual is regarded as responsible for her addiction.

The argument runs along these lines: If addiction is a disease, then in some ways it is out of our control and forecloses choices. A disease is a medical condition that develops outside of our control; it is, then, not a matter of choice. In the absence of choice, the addicted person is essentially relieved of responsibility. The addict has been overpowered by her addiction.

The counterargument describes addictive behavior as a choice. If people use alcohol and other drugs or engage in certain behaviors that lead to obvious problems, yet they continue to use or act out, then they are making choices to do so. Since those choices lead to addiction, blame and responsibility clearly rest on the addict's shoulders. It then becomes more a matter of free will and our free will motivates or authorizes the actions we have chosen.

Recent scientific studies on the biochemical responses of the brain are tipping the scales toward the more deterministic view of addiction as a disease. They appear to show that the structure of the brain's reward system combined with certain biochemical responses and certain environments cause people to become addicted. The disease drives the choices individuals make.

In such studies, and in media reports, the term "the hijacked brain" is often used, along with other language that emphasizes the addict's lack of choice in the matter. Sometimes the pleasure-reward system has been "commandeered." Other times it "goes rogue."

These expressions are accompanied by the conclusion that there are "addicted brains." Also the word "hijacked" is especially evocative; people often have a visceral reaction to it, which is precisely why this term is becoming more commonly used in connection with addiction. It is important to be aware of the effects of such language on our understanding.

When most people think of a hijacking, they picture a person, sometimes wearing a mask and always wielding some sort of a weapon, who takes control of a car, plane, or train. The hijacker may not drive or pilot the vehicle himself, but the violence involved leaves no doubt as to who is in charge. Someone can hijack a vehicle for a variety of reasons, but mostly it boils down to needing to escape or wanting to use the vehicle itself as a weapon in a greater plan. Hijacking is a means to an end; it is always and only oriented to the goals of the hijacker. Innocent victims are ripped from their normal lives by the violent intrusion of the hijacker.

In the "hijacked" view of addiction, the brain is the innocent victim of certain substances—alcohol, cocaine, nicotine, or heroin, for example—as well as certain behaviors like eating, gambling, or sexual activity. The drugs or the neurochemicals produced by the behaviors overpower and redirect the brain's normal responses, and thus take control of (hijack) it. For addicted people, that martini or cigarette is the weapon-wielding hijacker who is going to compel certain behaviors.

To do this, drugs like alcohol and cocaine, and behaviors like gambling, light up the brain's pleasure circuitry, often bringing a burst of euphoria. Other studies indicate that people who are addicted have lower dopamine and serotonin levels in their brains, which means that it takes more of a particular substance or behavior for them to experience pleasure or to reach a certain threshold of pleasure. People tend to want to maximize pleasure; we tend to do things that give us more of it. There's logic at work. If four drinks make me feel great, fourteen drinks will be amazing. We also tend to chase the high when it subsides, trying hard to recreate the same level of pleasure we experienced in the past. It is not uncommon to hear addicts talk about wanting to experience the euphoria of a first high. Often they never reach it again but keep trying anyway. All of this lends credence to the description of the brain as hijacked. The hijacked brain isn't capable of making good or reasonable choices because it isn't in charge anymore.

Analogies and comparisons can be effective and powerful tools in explanation, especially when the objects compared are not obviously similar at first glance. A comparison can be especially compelling when one of the objects is familiar or common and is wrested from its usual context. Similarities shared between disparate cases can help highlight features in each that might otherwise escape notice. But analogies and comparisons always break down at some point, often when the differences are seen to be greater than the similarities. This is the case with understanding addiction as hijacking.

A hijacker comes from outside and takes control by violent means. A hijacker takes a vehicle that is not his; hijacking is always a form of stealing and kidnapping. A hijacker always takes someone else's vehicle; you cannot hijack your own car. That is a type of nonsense or category mistake. Ludwig Wittgenstein offered that money passed from your left hand to your right is not a gift.[16] The practical consequences of this action are not the same as those of a gift. Writing yourself a thank you note would be absurd.

The analogy of addiction and hijacking involves the same category mistake as the money switched from hand to hand. You can treat yourself poorly, callously, indifferently, or violently. In such cases, we might say the person is engaging in acts of self-abuse and self-harm. People self-sabotage in all sorts of creative and effective ways. Self-abuse can involve acting in ways that you know are not in your best interest in some larger sense or contrary to your desires. Self-abuse can land a person in all sorts of situations she'd rather avoid. This, however, is not hijacking; the practical consequences are quite different.

It might be tempting to claim that in an addiction scenario, the substance or behavior are the hijackers. However, those substances and behaviors need to be done by the person herself (barring cases in which someone is given drugs and may be made chemically dependent). In the usual cases, an individual is the one putting chemicals into her body or engaging in certain behaviors in the hopes of experiencing a certain feeling. This simply pushes the question back to whether a person can hijack herself.

There is a kind of intentionality to hijacking that clearly is absent in addiction. There's no accidental and unintentional "oops" in hijacking, however. Hijacking involves conceiving a plan and implementing it. It is true that those plans may be made up quickly, but a quick plan is still a plan. No one plans to become an addict. One certainly may plan to drink in reckless or dangerous ways but not with the intention of becoming an addict somewhere down the road. Addiction develops over time and requires repeated and worsening use.

In a hijacking situation, it is very easy to assign blame and responsibility. The villain is easy to identify. So are the victims—people who have had the bad luck of being in the wrong place at the wrong time. Even though they may continue to drive the car, hijacked people are given no real choice in the matter. They are coerced, so their responsibility is significantly if not completely mitigated. They are not responsible in the ways the hijackers are.

This is the heart of the matter. The hijacking analogy only makes sense against the view that addiction is either a choice or a disease. But a little logic is helpful here, since the "choice or disease" view rests on a false dilemma: this fallacy posits that only two options exist. Since there are only two options, they must be mutually exclusive. If we think, however, of addiction as involving both choice *and* disease, our outlook is likely to become more nuanced. For instance, the progression of many medical diseases is affected by the choices that individuals make. A patient who knows he has Chronic Obstructive Pulmonary Disease (COPD) and refuses to wear a respirator or at least a mask while using noxious chemicals is making a choice that exacerbates his condition. A person who knows he meets the DSM-5 criteria for substance use disorder, and still continues to use drugs, is making a choice and bears responsibility for it.

Linking choice and responsibility occurs in a wide range of cases. When choices are truly voluntary and made with appropriate knowledge, a person bears responsibility for those choices. If, out of boredom, I choose to toss lighted matches in the living room and it catches fire, I am responsible. If I choose to cheat on my taxes, I am responsible.

However, there are many ways choices can be constrained. Being a victim of a hijacking is one extreme time of constraint put on choices. Explicit and overt coercion always constrains choice. But we must also acknowledge that choice can be constrained in ways other than by force or overt coercion. There is no doubt that the choices of people progressing to addiction are constrained; compulsion and impulsiveness constrain choices. Many addicts will say they choose to take that first drink or drug, and once they start, they cannot stop. A classic binge drinker is a prime example: his choices are constrained with the first drink. He both has and does not have a choice. (That moment before the first drink or drug is what the philosopher Owen Flanagan describes as a "zone of control.") But he still bears some degree of responsibility to others and to himself.[17]

The complexity of each person's experience with addiction should caution us to avoid false quandaries, such as the one that requires us to define addiction as either disease or choice. Accepting the view that addiction is either one or the other carries some very distorted and simplistic views about responsibility. We need to continue to create more nuanced conceptions of addiction and recovery along with conceptions of choice, free will, and responsibility. Addicts are neither hijackers nor victims, and it is time to retire this analogy.

Chapter Six

FORMS OF LIFE: ADDICTS ARE FROM MARS AND NONADDICTS FROM PLUTO

IT DOES SEEM ADDICTS AND NONADDICTS DON'T—AND CAN'T—THINK IN THE same ways. Addicts operate in the world with a different logic from nonaddicts, which leads to significant comprehension problems. It is as if we all didn't share the same world or form of life. The expression, "form of life," comes from Ludwig Wittgenstein and can help us understand why there are comprehension problems and how they can be overcome.

Wittgenstein uses "form of life" in two different, though not unrelated, ways.[18] The first way is to mark the differences between human beings and other animals. Canine, bovine, feline, and so on all pick out a natural kind, each of which is different from the others and different from us homo sapiens. Wittgenstein has no desire to argue that humans are superior or the only animals that use language. Rather, he is trying to mark what we humans *do*, and one way to do this is to make comparisons to other animals. But one of his points is that even if a lion, for example, *could* speak, we would not understand it because we don't experience the world in the same way as a lion because we are so physiologically different.[19] So whatever language a lion uses isn't comprehensible to us. The best we can do is imagine or project what we think the animal is saying or conveying. Ask any pet owner if he does this.

Wittgenstein also uses the expression "form of life" to mark different ways of life, ways of living, or worldviews within human beings. Evolutionary biologists and fundamentalist Christians, for example, have two different forms of life. Forms of life differ from one another in terms of their framework conditions, which both make possible and limit the range of what makes sense and what is meaningful. Consider an evolutionary biologist and a religious fundamentalist. Where the scientist views the earth and its inhabitants as products of evolution extending over millions of years, with mutations and adaptations as the driving force, a religious fundamentalist sees God's authorship and workmanship. Evolutionary biologists and fundamentalists see the same chimpanzee sitting in the cage before them, but in another important way, they do not. That chimp *means* very different things to biologists and fundamentalists.

Framework conditions are public and shared; we do not construct them for ourselves. Nor does one consciously choose the most basic or fundamental frameworks. Rather, Wittgenstein says, we are trained or enculturated into worldviews. We learn behaviors and learn to value some things while devaluing others. We come to closely identify with particular practices and values, and they become fused with our identity. These worldviews comprise the scaffolding of our thoughts; they shape the intelligibility and meaning of our experiences. The biologist may not be able to entertain—never mind conceive—the possibility that there is some sort of divine authorship. The religious fundamentalist, too, may be incapable of conceiving the alternative that humans share ancestry with apes. However, it is the acceptance of some frameworks that may later enable us to intentionally choose other frameworks. Some scientists find God while some religious people lose their faith and adopt more secular frameworks.

Active addicts have a form of life that is different from that of recovering addicts as well as different from that of nonaddicts. In many ways, the world we all share is the same in important respects, but, in some deep ways, the world and its meanings are as radically different for the active addict, the nonaddict, and the recovering addict as they are for the evolutionary biologist and the religious fundamentalist. Living in alternative forms of life may lead to comprehension problems, which is certainly true for active addicts, recovering addicts, and nonaddicts. These problems are not insurmountable in principle, though there may some challenges on a practical level.

These different forms of life and the identities they create are not completely separate from each other. There are places where the boundaries between them become blurry and more permeable. People who inhabit the edge or margin of one form of life may find themselves crossing the border or even moving back and forth. Or, perhaps just as likely, the border itself moves. This entails that the categories of active addict, recovering addict, and nonaddict are not hard and fast. This isn't surprising given that substance use disorders are along a spectrum; a person's identity or group membership may change as she progresses down the spectrum toward more severe or as she moves back toward more moderate use. These categories are even fuzzier with people who suffer from more than one addiction. Perhaps one addiction is well managed while another is worsening.

An active alcoholic may see the glass of scotch on the table as something he deserves and that will help wipe away his problems. The nonalcoholic sees it as something he can take or leave. The recovering alcoholic sees it as a reminder of how he was and how he might become again were he to drink it. It is the same glass of scotch sitting on the table, yet it's not.

Addicts may be almost entirely enigmatic to nonaddicts. A nonaddict may just not understand those of us who would risk our livelihoods, families, and whatever else we hold near and dear in order to use our drugs of choice. As a therapist once said to me, "Why don't you just cut down on your drinking?" She couldn't see that that wasn't a viable option for me at the time. What is possible for one person may be impossible for another.

We addicts can also justify, rationalize, minimize, and deny when it helps to preserve our worldviews. We may claim to be only experimenting or using less dangerous drugs. We may cite a legitimate medical condition all the while misrepresenting how often we're taking prescription pain medications. In a sense, addicts are dogmatic; we tend to hold on to our views no matter how much counter evidence or other arguments are offered. As addictions progress, some people are more willing to lose, cut off, or be cut off from people who challenge our behaviors and, by extension, our worldviews. With others who share our same addictions, we make a certain sense. One gambler who has lost almost all his money but is willing to let the remainder ride in the belief that *he will win this time* makes sense to another gambler. To nonaddicts, unless they've been enlisted in enabling us, we may prove to be beyond their logic and sanity. No amount of persuasive argument may work with us; we can talk past each other for perpetuity.

Now consider some differences between people in long-term recovery and those who are in active addiction or newly entering a recovery program. Some new people are in recovery programs not voluntarily but because of a court mandate. They may have no desire to stop their use but only a desire to fulfill the minimal legal obligation and never be caught again. Other new people genuinely want to stop using but often assume that without their drug or behavior of choice, life is going to be boring, predictable, and, quite importantly, not fun. They cannot imagine never using again for the rest of their lives. New people often judge those who go to meetings and share their stories or feelings as a bunch of losers. People in recovery may view those same people as helping to save lives. Active addicts and addicts in recovery see the same people sitting in those chairs, but in many ways, they don't.

An active addict or one newly in recovery often cannot understand the recovering addict who says, "Your life will be better when you do not drink. You will like yourself more. Others will like you more. You will have more friends and a lot more fun." To the unrecovered, people in recovery can seem preachy and sanctimonious. Early on, no matter how many times and in how many ways an old-timer says that life can be better, more fun, rewarding, and so on, what the new person hears is, "Blah, blah, serenity. Blah, blah, blah, serenity."

There may be significant comprehension problems between addicted populations as well. An alcoholic may not understand sex addiction while the sex addict may not understand food addiction, and the food addict cannot make sense of someone who would be addicted to heroin. There's more "blah blah" happening here.

So, how does "blah blah" become something intelligible to the active or newly recovering addicts? How do people with different addictions come to understand people with other addictions? And how do active addicts understand people in recovery? How do nonaddicts come to understand addicts? These comprehension gaps aren't unbridgeable, which is the good news. Forms of life are not discrete and disconnected from one another. Rather, they overlap and crisscross and, importantly, share the same background of the human form of life. This is why problems of comprehension are not insurmountable even when we encounter people who are radically different from us.

It is important to recognize a certain asymmetry between people active in their addictions and people in recovery. People in recovery do understand active addicts and those who are not in recovery for the very simple reason that they have been there and have shared similar experiences. This is not to say that addicts are all the same or share one defining trait or attribute. But there are some commonalities that provide the necessary material for crossing the comprehension gap.

Wittgenstein's concept of "family resemblance" offers a powerful tool for bridging these gaps. He introduces the concept as an alternative to assuming that there must be one trait that all members of a particular category share.[20] His example is games: It is not possible to find the common denominator between chess, tennis, Candy Land, foursquare, and solitaire even though each of these is called a game. There is no one common trait. Instead, there are patterns and weaves.

My brother and I don't look alike in easily identifiable ways. A quick glance or even a good long stare would not reveal we're related. Closer examination shows we have similar hand gestures, laugh lines that run in the same direction, and mouths that crack into similar smiles. It isn't one feature that makes us similar but rather that there are crisscrossing and overlapping traits and behaviors between us. I might have my father's build, my grandmother's eye color, and my mother's ears. My brother may have our mother's build, our grandfather's hair color, and our father's eye color. Put us in a photo with all these others, and there isn't a single trait we all share but a series of traits that create a pattern. What we have in common is that we are part of the pattern.

The concept of family resemblance helps create a mutual intelligibility between active addicts and nonaddicts. Even for people whose addictions developed early in life, there was still a time when they were not yet addicted. While it may be difficult to recall those times, there is enough there to serve as a glimpse of how life could be without addictive drugs or behaviors. Nonaddicts may also see traits in their own behaviors that are similar in kind, but very different in degree, from those of the person struggling with an addiction. Most people experience times in their lives when too much feels out of control, and they need and want some relief. The needs and wants may be similar to those of an addict, but the means to meet them will be very different. In that moment of recognizing the shared needs and wants, there may be a flash of comprehension and compassion for the addict by the nonaddict.

The concept of family resemblance is most powerful for people with active addictions and people in recovery. These similarities and crisscrossings are behaviors, attitudes, and experiences. I may not have been arrested for drunk driving, but I was willing to risk expulsion from school like you did. Someone else may have engaged in all sorts of risky sexual behaviors while another regularly forgot or didn't bother to eat since she was too busy drinking. Someone else passed out regularly and woke up in places completely unfamiliar to her. Yet another didn't pass out but would spend hours riding public transportation. Some people remained remarkably high functioning in their addictions while others lost it all very quickly.

Sit among any group of people talking about their addictions, and one of the most common refrains is, "I didn't do that exactly, but I did . . ." Cataloguing all these behaviors and experiences is not possible but not because there are too many to count. Rather, they are impossible to count because they blur and blend into each other and cannot be separated.

The family resemblance approach encourages looking for complexities and patterns over one condition or criterion. Most people who struggle with addictive substances and behaviors will never have a brain scan to show what's happening in their brain's reward system. Many people will identify as addicted without any legal or medical intervention. The self-identification often comes from assessing and comparing one's behavior to one's own past behavior and that of others. A person can begin to see similarities in the stories of others. She may come to see herself as sharing many threads in a broader weave. The recognition that comes from a family resemblance approach may be one of the earliest steps a person takes in naming her condition, understanding, and then transforming herself.

Chapter Seven

THE TRAIN'S ONLY STOP IS TERMINAL UNIQUENESS

As addicts we often isolate ourselves even if at times we are the life of the party. We may want to appear to be the life of the party, but many of us spend an enormous amount of time hiding in plain sight. Our thoughts tend to run down "the terminal uniqueness" track to the land of NUM (Nobody Understands Me). Who else could possibly understand my life and all its challenges? No one can understand how hard it is to be me. I myself cannot even understand how hard it is! If my starting point is that no one can understand me, I have no reason to reach out to others and try and make them genuinely understand me. Nor do I see any reason to try to understand another, for she will be as enigmatic and opaque to me as I am to her. But yet, we addicts spend much of our time comparing our insides to the outsides of others.

This question of how each of us can understand others— what is going on in their minds, what they are thinking, how they see the world or experience pain—is what philosophers call "the problem of other minds," and it has been a particularly vexing one. It is usually framed along these lines: I have total access to what is in my mind, and it is hidden from the view of others. No one can look into my mind and see that I am having the thought, "My gosh those are ugly shoes that woman is wearing." I can be thinking that, all the while saying to her, "Those shoes are fantastic." My thoughts have a certain inviolable privacy: they are mine and no one can have access to them. I've got privileged access to the contents of my mind. My mind and its contents are impenetrable unless I make those thoughts public in shared language. So, the picture is that each of us is a little self-contained privacy unit that engages and interacts with others by means of a shared language. The private comes first, and then the public language arises for sharing the private.

Many active addicts regularly subscribe to this picture, and even recovering ones remain susceptible to its allure. We crave our privacy and can go to any length to keep people at a great remove. We are remarkably adept at hiding, which makes a lot of sense: We may fear embarrassment or shame about public exposure of our addictive behaviors. This is particularly true of people who manage to hide their use for a long time. We might lose a job or our status in a community. We want to be "normal" like everyone else. If we can just somehow pass as normal, for instance if we can drink socially or perhaps not at all with social drinkers, they will have no clue. In fact, they may be shocked when we later tell them about our addiction. Sometimes they try to convince us that we can't be a real addict since, to their way of thinking, we were all drinking in the same ways. All the while we were wearing masks, and we know the truth that our drinking is not normal. Once people catch on to us or are able to see behind the mask, our go-to move is to avoid them. We are driven by the fear of discovery by others.

Even more interesting are the ways addicts try to hide from themselves. This is a difficult dynamic to reconcile with the assumption about privacy and privileged access that undergirds the problem of other minds. The common assumption is that with the privileged access to the contents of one's own mind comes a guarantee that one could never be wrong about that content. This is the argument Descartes made in the mid-1600s in his quest for absolute certainty when he claimed to be able to clearly apprehend the total contents of his mind.[21] He claimed to see every idea he had in his mind and thus "introspection," or looking inward, became the primary model for self-knowledge. With privileged access, no one else has access to what is happening in my mind, so I'm the only one who has the perspective and authority to say what is going through my mind. This raises two questions. First, can I really know the truth but willfully ignore it? Second, can I ever be wrong about what is going on in my mind?

Knowing but willfully ignoring the truth is a common dynamic. It embodies the classic "Yeah, but . . . " approach. For example, I know that I really do not want to undertake a new project right now. I do not have the focus or the desire to dedicate the time it takes to produce a quality work. I know this about myself right now, but I still embark upon the project. Several weeks later, when I am miserable and my work falls so far below my own standards that I can barely glimpse it, I can be full of recrimination and regret. Yes, I knew I did not want to do this, but I did it anyway. Some of us are constantly overriding what we know about ourselves, and the incentives to do so can be high. The rewards can be higher still. Sooner or later, however, the payment comes due.

The easiest way to get at this dynamic is when people say, "Yes, I knew it (a problem with substances, relationship dynamics, etc.) was bad but I did not *know know* it." The *know know* is crucial. Self-knowledge is often something far different from, and greater than, being able to admit that something is bad or wrong; that is a very thin sort of knowledge.

The issue isn't that "you know that," but rather that you know how to do something with that knowledge. Consider: I know that "E=mc,²" but I don't really know how to do anything with that knowledge. On a physics exam, I would not be able to "show my work." I could write the sentence but not do much with the formula. So, I know it, but I don't *know know* it. And perhaps this does come down to the adage that it isn't just about talking the talk, because talk is cheap after all. Rather, it is walking the walk; it is a matter of doing something with the knowledge. Knowledge that isn't put into practice is like an ornamental knob that spins but doesn't engage with anything. Pretty, perhaps, but useless in some fundamental ways.

Perhaps it's beneficial to replace *know know* with "know how and will do." How often do any of us say, "I know I should stop and I will when . . . " and go on to list a long chain of conditions? The promise made today to change tomorrow is easy to make but hard to keep. This is a form of procrastination, which is a form of self-deception.

Procrastination is a failure of the relationship between knowledge and the will, according to Kierkegaard. Knowledge should guide our actions, but when we know what we should do but are unwilling, even for a moment, a gap opens. A quick-as-a-wink moment of hesitation can grow into a long period of inaction. Procrastination is deceptive because it can masquerade as activity. We can tell ourselves that we are gathering more information, getting other affairs into order, making arrangements, and so on. We can keep turning all the considerations we can possibly identify over in our minds, repeatedly—"paralysis by analysis." Procrastination is like sewing without tying a knot at the end of the thread. One goes through the motions but one doesn't actually sew. The practical consequences are quite different.[22]

The case of being wrong about what you know in your own mind is pretty common. Addicts often describe their minds as being places where one wouldn't want to go alone. It is a "bad neighborhood" with all sorts of decrepit and condemned buildings and trash-strewn sidewalks. Descartes's mind, by contrast, is a beautifully planned suburban community with lovely rolling lawns and no sidewalks. It is probably gated, too. I'm often wrong about what I'm thinking in part because my thinking is influenced by my feelings and physical condition. Addicts regularly suggest that people should not make decisions to undertake a course of action when they are Hungry, Angry, Lonely, or Tired—the recommendation is to HALT. I regularly get it wrong about what I need or want from another person when I'm tired. I easily take offense when none is intended when I feel angry about something. I am Crabby Appleton when I'm hungry; I become a different person from my more usual, easygoing self. These are the easy cases.

However, the more difficult cases are the ones where self-deception and denial are in full swing. The minds of addicts are dark places, for all sorts of self-protective reasons. We do not want parts of ourselves to come to light. This light imagery is powerful and comes from the 1600s, when Descartes and others argued that the light of reason, when applied well, can lead to knowledge that reveals the great truths of nature, and perhaps even the nature of God.[23] The expression, "a light bulb went on," reveals how we commonly think of knowledge as light. Light illuminates, whereas darkness lends itself to hiding. Denial is an important mechanism for snuffing out light. Denial means that we keep things from ourselves, often by rationalizing—an addict's second best friend after her drug or behavior of choice. We tell ourselves, "I can't be an addict because I have a good job," or "So-and-so is an addict and he drank a lot worse than I ever did." Denial and self-deception go together. Where denial is able to run at full speed, I will be deceived about what I can claim to know about myself. I have such an investment in preserving a view of myself, for example, that I cannot even entertain the possibility that things may not be as they appear to me to be (and perhaps only to me).

Denial and self-deception consume enormous amounts of energy. A person who is busy hiding from herself has no real desire to know herself, and perhaps will spend more time polishing her outward appearance. If good recovery groups show us anything, it's the difficulty of hiding from yourself when you're surrounded by people who share similar experiences. It's also harder to hide and isolate from others. It turns out people are not so mysterious to each other after all. The allure of terminal uniqueness is lessened as we begin to recognize the elements of family resemblances that crisscross. This recognition diminishes the need for willful ignorance and provides fodder for people to understand what is really going on in their minds.

In order to recognize similarities, we must first pay attention to people and the world around us. While it is true that people can wear masks and be quite adept at hiding what they're really thinking or feeling, more often than not we can have a pretty good idea of what's going on with someone. Do you really need to look into someone else's mind to ascertain that someone is grief stricken? In many cases, as Wittgenstein points out, you can see the grief written on someone's face; grief is personified in the face.[24] You can see emotion in the eyes, on the brow, in the way a person holds her head, and in the clutching of her hands. You can see doubt race across someone's face. You can see surprise in the movement of someone's head.

So, we don't need to see *inside* someone's head, and we don't need someone to look inside ours. We need to see faces and learn how to read. To see these things and have them register as information, we have to be awake and alert—physically, intellectually, and emotionally. In our addicted states, we could not be present to other people. It was all about us, and then we made the mistaken assumption that other people would be similarly self-absorbed. Once we are awake—and a good, proactive relationship to our recovery helps us stay awake—we cannot help but see that many people can understand us, and we them. It is a relief to get off the train that stops only at terminal uniqueness.

Chapter Eight

STORIES, CONNECTIONS, AND BAD LOGIC

TELLING AND LISTENING TO STORIES IS ONE OF THE MOST important ways people begin to identify as having an addiction and committing to recovery. The narrative each person tells herself and others is a big part of how we construct our self-identities. It is how we begin to make sense of our past and present and understand our hopes for the future. In constructing our narratives, we identify which particular events or experiences were formative or transformative. It is a way to indicate that some experiences really matter to how we see ourselves now and how we hope to change in the future. In telling our stories to others, we also assume ownership of our experiences and their meaning. Each of us is able to stake a claim to having a certain authority or legitimate perspective on ourselves. Of course, this authority is neither absolute nor infallible.

We often reinterpret experiences in light of new ones or in light of the experiences, insight, and guidance of others. We sometimes come to see that we were wrong or inaccurate about something when we hear other people saying the same things. In our minds, a belief may make complete sense, but when other people say it aloud, our laughter with others provides great comfort and relief. Telling our stories means opening up to others, while giving away pieces of ourselves, and getting much in return.

In taking ownership of our experiences, actions, beliefs, and values and creating a narrative about ourselves, we must take responsibility. Rights and responsibilities are flip sides of the same coin. We share stories about ourselves and our experiences in the hope that they will be helpful to other people. They also serve as reminders to ourselves. In telling our stories and hearing different verses of the same song in others' stories, we may gradually see that we, too, are addicted. Incorporating that fact into part of our identity is a momentous occasion. Many people who later identify as addicts remember two life-altering events in a great detail: The first is when they first used, and the second is when they recognized and accepted that they were an addict.

Given the importance of stories we tell about ourselves and how they shape our identities, I need to tell some of mine. It isn't so different from the stories of other alcoholics or addicts, and this realization is a comfort. No need to suffer the ill effects of terminal uniqueness. My story does reveal some of my own bad logic that is shared with many who struggled to name their addictions.

How we tell our stories matters enormously. We can tell them in a misleading or defensive way. If we are too concerned with how we appear to others, we shade the truth; we edit out pieces that are less than flattering. We may overinflate certain parts to cast ourselves in a better light. Of course, there are always omissions in the stories we tell; it just isn't possible to remember every detail. Unintentional omissions are different from deliberate ones. The stories that are most helpful to ourselves and others are the ones told honestly and in a genuine spirit of humility.

The cheat sheet version of my addiction, sobriety, and recovery is that beginning in high school, and continuing through college, I was a regular blackout and pass-out drinker. My drinking career comprised eight years of extreme binging peppered with unsuccessful attempts to stop. I played a lot of tennis. A lot. It was both my refuge and my special torment that helped to fuel and was fueled by my alcohol consumption.

I was a slacker in high school and barely did any work. In college, I became a high functioning, cyclically drunk and hung-over worker bee who fell in love with philosophy. When graduation rolled around, I had no job and no plan. I almost felt surprised I was graduating.

I was nearly killed in a car accident a few months after graduation. I had not been drinking but would've been a couple of hours later. In the hospital, while being offered what seemed to me a sampler platter of narcotics, I had the distinct thought, "Betty Ford, here I come." I declined all the narcotic offerings and once out of the hospital felt too emotionally flat-lined to even drink. After a few weeks, I decided to see how long I could go *not drinking*. I considered it an experiment, which, thankfully, has lasted more than twenty-seven years.

My relationship to my own recovery continues to evolve. What worked five, ten, and twenty years ago may not work so well today. I am a different person now, so I need different things in my recovery. After more than twenty years, which were quite good and happy on any accounting, I'd say I finally made a passionate commitment to living a life of recovery.

Part of the reason I drank was that I felt so different from my friends. Catholic high school in the early 1980s was not a great place to come out as a lesbian. My strategy was to drink to feel more comfortable so that I could convince myself that I fit in. It wasn't effective because I drank with a vengeance, which was different from my friends. It just made me different in yet another way, which further fueled my drinking. Drinking was never an effective strategy, yet I stuck with it expecting I would eventually be able to master it.

In college, I fell in love with both tennis and squash. Give me a racquet and I pick up the game instantly. I promised myself that I wouldn't drink during my athletic seasons. I did it to varying degrees of success, buying the lie that my not drinking in season was the truth. Never mind that at the end of each season I would start drinking and often not stop until I passed out. That didn't count as evidence for anything. At one point, I willed myself to believe that drinking to the point of blacking or passing out was the exception for me, not the norm. My stopping drinking for months on end convinced me that I didn't have a problem. I put the logic I learned in my philosophy courses to good use and came up with the following argument:

1. If I am not an alcoholic (antecedent), then I can stop drinking (consequent).

2. I can stop drinking (consequent).

3. Therefore, I am not an alcoholic (antecedent).

This argument commits what we call "The Fallacy of Affirming the Consequent." An "if . . . then" statement is called a conditional and is about the order of two events. The antecedent happens first and is followed by the consequent. The fallacy assumes that the order of the two events can be reversed and still be true. Consider this argument, which commits the same fallacy:

1. If the president vetoes the bill, the bill fails.

2. The bill fails.

3. Therefore, the president vetoed the bill.

A bill may fail for one of several reasons. It may never make it out of committee; the House could vote it down, as could the Senate. A bill will always fail after a President vetoes it. (Yes, a veto can be overridden, but that's a separate issue.)

Back to my drinking argument: I *could* stop drinking for periods of time; I'd stop when I was in season. I'd also stop drinking when I was around my parents (or at least limit myself to two beers, which didn't really count as drinking). Clearly I was shading the definition of not drinking. I was also ignoring any consideration about the duration of not drinking. The "not drinking" was what mattered. The "not staying stopped" and starting up again didn't count as evidence of anything. To see the fallacy at its extreme, consider a person who stops drinking every night because she passes out. Although she does stop drinking, it is not justified to conclude that she is not an alcoholic.

When I wasn't engaging in bad logic, I was busy reading the ancient Greek philosophers. My second early philosophizing about my drinking "problem" was aided and abetted by Aristotle. The only way I could make sense of my drinking—which I knew in my gut to be alcoholism, even if I tried to deny it—was a matter of my suffering from weakness of will, which Aristotle termed, "akrasia." My drinking was a product of my own akrasia; I was the author of my moral failure.

As Aristotle describes it, akrasia is a chronic condition that has two versions. The first is impetuosity where one acts rashly under the influence of the passions. There is no deliberation and no use of reason; one is a slave to one's appetites and emotions. The second version involves deliberation and the use of reason to identify what the good, prudent, or healthy choice would be, but one still gives in to the passions. One acts under the influence of the passions. A person knows what she should do, but she still doesn't do it. For Aristotle, this type of akrasia is the worse of the two.[25] I suffered from both forms of akrasia at different times in my drinking career. That is not to say that akrasia was the cause of my addiction, although it may have aided and abetted it.

There's no escaping logic. After many years in recovery, a new argument about my drinking or not drinking entered the scene. Lurking behind the question, "Why, after more than twenty-seven years of not drinking, do you still call yourself an alcoholic?" is a logical argument. This argument looks like this:

1. Alcoholics are people who drink.

2. You do not drink.

3. Therefore, you are not an alcoholic.

Some people wonder why I flip back and forth between saying, "I am an alcoholic" and "I am a recovering alcoholic." There is a world of difference between the two, isn't there? For me, and I say this only for myself, "alcoholic" is an identity conferring term that I live every day of my life. It is as much a part of my identity as being a lesbian. Do I stop being a lesbian if I am not in a relationship with someone? I don't think so, and I don't think that most heterosexuals would say they cease to be heterosexual when they are not in a relationship. The notion of relationship holds the key for why I identify as an alcoholic.

My identity as an alcoholic is not only based on my past experience with, or relationship to, alcohol but with my present and possible future ones as well. Not consuming alcohol is a relationship to alcohol. Imagining what my relationship to alcohol might be if I were to start drinking again is a relationship to alcohol. Writing an essay about my relationship to alcohol is a relationship to alcohol.

Imagination is powerful, and often we base our decisions on imagination more than actual knowledge and evidence. My decision not to drink because I understand myself as "still alcoholic" is based on weighing the potential costs and benefits of drinking compared to those of living a good and happy life.

This cost benefit approach is a version of what philosophers call "Pascal's Wager." Blaise Pascal (1623–1662) was a French philosopher, mathematician, and inventor. While he grappled with all sorts of issues, one of the most pressing of his time was the possibility of proving God's existence. Was such a proof possible? In the context of this question, Pascal offered several considerations that take the form of a wager or bet. The wager looks something like this:

> Assume there is no satisfactory evidence for God's existence. Is it still rational to believe in God? The expected value of believing in God is far greater than not believing in God. If one believed in God and acted in accordance with that belief and it turned out that God existed, one would win incalculably good things (Heaven, salvation, eternal life, and so on). If one believed in God and the belief turned out to be false, then one wouldn't really lose anything and the cost of believing would be really quite low. Therefore, it is rational to believe in God and live one's life in accordance with that belief.[26]

In the same vein, I imagine what it would be like to start drinking again. There may well be some pleasure. It would be fun to go out after work and have a few beers. Hearing the crack and fizzle when opening a bottle is itself a pleasure. The first swig of an ice-cold beer is refreshing. And then a nice buzz follows. I might even feel "normal" (whatever that means). In my imagination, I can go down that path. I can be just like those happy people we see in the commercials.

I cannot say with absolute certainty that I would go back to drinking the way I did before I quit the last time. There can't be certainty with a possibility. At best there may be probability, but then I appeal to past behavior. Before I stopped in 1987, I had tried quitting many times before and had failed miserably. As Mark Twain supposedly said, "Giving up smoking is the easiest thing in the world. I know because I have done it thousands of times." I don't know what would be true here. I have a list of failed attempts at not drinking against one long stint of not drinking. My not drinking may be a phase, albeit a very long phase at this point. Which way does the scale tip?

Still imagining my future possible drinking, I consider what I know about my own and other people's experiences. I can choose my comparison pool. There are those who engage in moderate use after periods of abuse. I might belong in that pool with my controlled drinking. In another comparison pool are those who "go back out" and report how their using quickly returned to where they had left off. Furthermore, their use quickly accelerated downhill, like a heavy truck without brakes or steering. But while this has been true for others, would it be true for me? I don't know. So how does the scale tip?

The expected value in believing that "I am still an alcoholic," and then acting from that belief by not drinking, is far greater than any alternative. There are at least three possible paths I could take.

On the first, I believe I am still alcoholic and do not drink, and it turns out I am wrong about that belief. In this case it has cost me very little. Perhaps I missed a little fun by not drinking, but that is a minor cost. It's a pretty good scenario. The scales tip toward happiness.

On the second, I believe I am no longer an alcoholic and start drinking again, and it turns out I am wrong in my belief. The costs in this case are devastatingly high. I could lose everything. This is the worst scenario, especially if I pick up where I left off, and my drinking gains momentum. The scales tip totally toward misery.

On the third, I believe I am still alcoholic and I don't drink, and it turns out that belief is right. In this scenario the expected value or gain is the highest. I have "incalculably good things" in my life since sobering up, including wonderful relationships with my family and friends and work that is rewarding. This is the best possible scenario, with the scales tipping totally toward happiness.

I conclude, therefore, that it is rational for me to believe that my alcoholism is alive and kicking, and I should live my life in accordance with that belief. I continue to pick the third option. Other people's stories play an important role in my continuing to choose this path. Hearing others describe how they thought they could handle drinking again, or others who did manage to handle it for some period of time, provides an important check against my belief that I, and my actions, would be different. "Handling drinking" is generally not how people who don't have a problem describe their relationship to alcohol. If I find myself concerned with "handling" my drinking, then that provides sufficient reason and motivation not to start up again.

Chapter Nine

WHY IS IT SO HARD TO TRUST YOURSELF?

People who don't trust themselves engage in second-guessing, waffling on their choices and decisions, and changing their courses of action. People lacking in self-trust often sabotage their own goals, dreams, and plans in creative ways; all of which are classic symptoms of a terrible malady.

When a person's lack of self-trust extends to most areas of her life, she may come to see herself as, and actually be, untrustworthy to herself. There are many reasons why and circumstances under which a person loses trust in herself. Addiction, especially, saps self-trust; not trusting oneself is a hallmark of addiction. We have good reasons and plenty of evidence for why we shouldn't trust ourselves, such as our histories that are replete with broken promises to ourselves and others. We say we will do one thing and then we veer in the exact opposite direction. We say we want something, yet we act in ways that will keep us from achieving it. Can we trust ourselves to act in our own best interest? The evidence points to a resounding "No" because we are so unreliable and untrustworthy.

Trust is an Aristotelian virtue.[27] It is a mean, a balance, between the two extremes of excess and deficiency. Having too much trust makes one gullible, where one will believe anything because someone says it. The gullible person trusts far beyond what is justified and prudent. The person who has an extreme lack of trust is paranoid in the sense of not accepting anything that anyone else claims. There are never good enough reasons to trust for such a person; all the evidence in the world would not suffice to warrant trust.

Trustworthiness is an abiding character state; trustworthiness is woven into the fabric of a person's being. A trustworthy person is someone who is reliable, consistent, and truthful in her actions across the board. With a trustworthy person, what you see is what you get. There are no hidden agendas. It's not that this person is perfect. Rather, her actions tend to spring from and reinforce the moral values and commitments she lives.

Judging the trustworthiness of others is not always an easy matter. The most successful con artists are the ones who appear to be most trustworthy, and they're able to dupe people who trust. There are criteria we can appeal to when deciding whether to trust someone or have faith in a state of affairs, but they come without guarantees. Sometimes the facts speak for themselves. I wouldn't trust a restaurant owner who has a list of health code violations. I wouldn't trust a financial planner with a track record of bad investments. I may trust that person for advice on other matters, though.

Part of what it means to be a mature and trusting person is to know when, where, to whom, and how far to extend our trust. We learn how to trust and sometimes, unfortunately, we learn the most when we misplace our trust. We gain the ability to recognize who is trustworthy and who isn't.

For people who love or depend on those who suffer from addiction, trust and trustworthiness present special challenges. Often the hope that another person will be trustworthy affects our ability to see her accurately. We see our hope rather than the degree of the person's actual trustworthiness. When a person makes too many mistakes judging the trustworthiness of others, she may start to question her own reliability. She may start to doubt herself.

When it comes to how much a person should trust *herself* and gauge her own trustworthiness, things get tricky. What could function as a standard or benchmark? Anything we might use is tainted or not good enough because it comes from within us. It gets even more difficult for people who are addicted because we may have such a long track record of our own unreliability.

Complicating the matter further is the belief that each person knows herself better than others possibly could. This goes back to the privileged access the "terminally unique" claim to have. On this view, each person has an access to her own beliefs, desires, thoughts, and emotions that no one else can have. Each of us can turn a light to even the darkest, most remote corners of our mind, but no one else can see those corners and what lurks there. On the basis of privileged access, each person can say, "I have the best perspective on who I am."

However, the relationship between privileged access and perspective is muddy, murky, and confounds the question of how much we should trust ourselves. Does each of us actually have enough distance to have perspective? Even with the best light, I may not be able to see myself clearly because I'm too close. I cannot read a printed page held too close to my face; I need to extend my arm. What is the equivalent of that arm stretch for seeing my own actions and my character?

Many addicts claim to have privileged access. We know the things we've done, and we believe that only people who are seriously warped, damaged, deranged, sick, and messed up could steal from our kid's savings or lick a filthy floor when someone dropped some cocaine. We know the ways in which we've been unreliable for others and for ourselves. Our claims to self-knowledge are often wrapped in self-loathing, which contribute to the lack of self-trust because it perversely heightens the belief in privileged access. At some point, we cross the line between not trusting ourselves on certain matters and not trusting ourselves at all. The less a person trusts herself and others, the less she is able to successfully live her life. Every aspect of living requires trust of some sort; we need it to navigate the world in some really basic ways. Without it, we may not be able to move at all.

A problem arises when a cousin of privileged access enters and swamps the scene. That cousin is "epistemic authority"—a philosophical expression for "authority that is rooted in knowledge." A physicist has epistemic authority on relativity, a tax attorney on the tax code, and an oncologist on cancer. Epistemic authority is rooted in knowledge and expertise in a particular area or subject matter.

Privileged access together with epistemic authority entails that each person is an expert on herself. This implies that a person could not possibly be wrong about herself. She knows herself better and more accurately than anyone else can know her. In a sense, each person has "insider knowledge" of herself. She knows that she may seethe within when someone unfairly criticizes her and yet maintain a calm façade. She may fantasize about revenge scenarios and witty retorts, but that is as far as she will go.

Here, too, there is something that seems right about the conclusion: I know my history, likes and dislikes, beliefs, values, commitments, and non-negotiables better than anyone else.

A dangerous extension happens when someone believes that a horrible set of truths resides in her and that she is the only one who really knows them. That's the privileged access piece of the puzzle. She may claim to know she is a rotten, miserable person because only a rotten, miserable person would have done the things she's done, or thought and felt the things she's thought and felt. She may even claim that this is her true self. She really knows herself to be a moral degenerate, for example, while others may see her in a nearly opposite way. That's the epistemic authority piece.

And here's where shame enters the picture. But first, let us differentiate shame from guilt. Both are moral emotions but with different objects and different scopes. Guilt usually attaches to a particular act, thought, or belief. Its scope is limited to that particular act or that class of acts. For example, I may feel guilty that I chose to attend a friend's party rather than visit an elderly relative. That act may belong to a class of acts in which I prioritize my pleasure over an obligation. My guilt is often a function of incongruence between what I want to do and what I have an obligation to do. Many addicts may feel guilt about some of their actions because they still see themselves as a good and trustworthy person. To assuage the guilt, they may rationalize or minimize the acts in questions. They take them to be the exception to the norm of their otherwise morally good behavior.

Shame, by contrast, doesn't attach to particular acts, thoughts, or feelings, but rather to the person as a whole. Under the right conditions, guilt transforms into shame. Guilt busts out of the particulars and becomes something amorphous that attaches to more and more, turning into shame, which is corrosive and spreads widely and deeply. A person ends up seeing everything about herself through the lens of shame. She becomes governed by shame and is ashamed of her very self.

Shame makes it difficult for a person to have an adequate perspective on herself. So, how well can a person rooted in shame know herself? It is, admittedly, a loaded question to ask. On the one hand, we have to acknowledge the authority each person can have about herself and her experiences. We live in a world in which some groups of people have been viewed as not having any epistemic authority on anything, including themselves. History is replete with examples of things being done to people in the name of their best interest or "for their own good," as well as for "the good of society." For example, approximately 20,000 people were forcibly sterilized in California between 1909 and 1963. The goal of the sterilization program was to keep people who were deemed "undesirable" from procreating so that the gene pool was not damaged. Conditions that warranted sterilization included alcoholism, prostitution, homelessness, and being poor.[28] To deny epistemic authority may be insulting, oppressive, and even dehumanizing.

But on the other hand, shame is a form of self-deception; it is one of the greatest hindrances to self-knowledge. Everything a person claims to know about herself has been strained through a thick filter of shame. Privileged access tells the person that she has the best perspective. No one else could have an accurate perspective on her, so whatever they have to offer is either wrong or worthless.

This dilemma has very pointy horns, and it's one with which many addicts wrestle. How can I come to know myself differently if I think I already know my terrible, ugly self fully? My shame will motivate me to keep those ugly truths hidden from others. Shame perpetuates a destructive and closed feedback cycle that reinforces the very shame that caused it to begin with.

One reason so many of us addicts tell our stories—whether in the context of a twelve-step program or group therapy, or with friends and family—is that we learn about ourselves by telling our story and by hearing other people's stories. This breaks open that closed feedback cycle. For example, hearing someone tell a story that has some significant similarity to mine can help me reframe my own understanding. What I have always seen as abject failure owing to my complete stupidity is, in another person, a combination of bad luck and circumstances well beyond anyone's control. Where one person may have felt she deserved everything bad that happened to her, another may respond with more empathy and compassion for herself.

Self-knowledge, it turns out, is deeply social. Introspection—looking inward—is a necessary, but not sufficient, condition for self-knowledge. How I see myself is certainly important, but I need to concede that others can see me and know me in ways that I cannot. I can learn about myself from others. This is true for all people but especially for those mired in shame.

One way back to self-trust, or one way of acquiring it for the first time, is through transforming shame into guilt because guilt can be addressed in more direct and effective ways. To feel guilt in the right direction and to the right degree is an enormous achievement. To feel guilt in this way is to have a sense of responsibility for your actions, beliefs, and values. To trust yourself is, in part, to know what is properly your responsibility and what is not. We can mediate guilt by taking responsibility.

Chapter Ten

"SHOULDING" ALL OVER YOURSELF

"Listen to me. I am shoulding all over myself."

—Stuart Smalley, "Stuart Saves His Family"[29]

BEFORE HE BECAME A US SENATOR FROM MINNESOTA, AL FRANKEN created the character of Stuart Smalley, first on *Saturday Night Live* and later in two movies. Smalley is the pinup boy for twelve-step programs, offering pithy statements when faced with any sort of adversity or challenge. His gentle humor reveals some of the most important truths in life.

Shoulding all over yourself can be a form of self-deception. We mistake "could" for "should." When we turn too many desires or possibilities into things we *should* or *must* do, we create misery that has a deep current of resentment. We may inflict this misery onto ourselves, but it often splashes onto others.

Our lives are governed by shoulds and oughts; they organize humans' lives. Immanuel Kant (1724–1804) offers two categories of oughts and shoulds in *Grounding for the Metaphysics of Morals*.[30] Kant calls oughts and shoulds imperatives, which are commands or demands. There are two kinds of oughts—hypothetical imperatives and categorical imperatives—that differ from each other based on when they are incumbent or have a hold on a person. Hypothetical imperatives have a hold on a person only when certain desires or goals are present. Categorical imperatives are moral commands that hold for all people regardless of their goals or desires.

A hypothetical imperative has the basic form, "If you want something of a particular sort, then you should undertake this action." There are two types of hypothetical imperatives that are directly related. This first Kant calls *counsels of prudence*. They're concerned with pursuing happiness or living a good life and are more like guidelines or advice for good overall living. The other type Kant identifies as *rules of skill*. These tell you what particular action you should take to realize your goals.[31]

The two types of hypothetical imperatives often intersect. I might believe that one way to live a good life is to regularly challenge myself to learn new things in order to avoid becoming too settled or stagnant. This is a counsel of prudence.[32] In light of this imperative, I set personal goals that are achievable with the right sort of effort and commitment; setting impossible goals only leads to feelings of failure. This is also a counsel of prudence. These two counsels of prudence govern my choice to learn taekwondo. Given this goal, rules of skill tell me that I must practice my kicks, punches, blocks, and patterns. I must also stretch because I am as flexible as a bronze statue.

The defining characteristic of hypothetical imperatives is their contingency—if you change your desire or understanding of a happy life, then your particular demands and oughts change. With hypothetical imperatives, the force of a should is contingent upon the desire, or the goals that reflect our desires; lose the desire and the power of the ought disappears. If I decide that my life is "good enough" and I don't need to challenge myself anymore, then there's no reason why I should continue with taekwondo or take up other new and challenging tasks.

Categorical imperatives, on the other hand, are moral demands that hold for all people universally, come what may. They allow no exceptions; they are absolute and universally binding on all people. A categorical imperative does not depend on having any particular goals and desires, including the desire to be a morally good person. Thus, a categorical imperative is never contingent in the way that hypothetical imperatives are.

Kant offers a rule he calls the *categorical imperative*.[33] When applied properly it will clearly and unambiguously produce what one must or must not do, and what one may or may not do. Its application tells us our moral duties, that is, our categorical imperatives. Kant offers three equivalent formulations of the categorical imperative that will always produce the same result. The first is, "Act only on that maxim through which you can at the same time will that it should become a universal law."[34] A maxim is an underlying rule or principle. In effect, Kant claims that whatever acts a person wills himself to do, he would also have to will that everyone else in the same circumstances would have to do the same. One example he offers is, "Lie when it suits your interest." It is impossible, Kant claims, for everyone to will that everyone else lie. There's a fundamental contradiction; lies only work when there is a presumption of truth. If everyone lied whenever they pleased, there would be no such thing as truth telling. Without truth, lies cannot work or be exposed. This formulation asks whether the act that you propose is one that everyone in similar circumstances could do.

The second formulation is, "Act in such a way that you treat the humanity, whether in your own person or any other person, always at the same time as an end, never merely as a means."[35] In other words, don't use yourself or others simply as tools to get what you want. The person who lies to his friend in order to get money is using his friend like an ATM machine. The lying friend treats the other as an object and doesn't respect the dignity of his friend.

Kant argues that reason alone underpins our moral system and provides motivation to act. Reason is the only motivating force that has moral value; sentiments or emotions play no role in determining our moral duties. Our reason tells us what we are morally required to do. We have a duty never to lie and a duty never to commit suicide. Additionally, Kant offers that one ought to develop some of one's talents and that one ought to help others sometimes. These are duties we all have to ourselves or to others.

Kant would agree that we ought to "should all over ourselves" when it comes to categorical imperatives because part of what it means to be human is to perform our moral duties. Kant claims we are most free when we give and then act out of the moral law. Kant's expression, which is in part how he frames the third formulation of the categorical imperative, is that we are "self-legislating members of the kingdom of ends."[36]

Categorical imperatives should always take precedence over hypothetical ones because absolute demands allow for no exception and hold true for all. Hypothetical imperatives are contingent, which doesn't mean they're not important—they are, but not important enough to have priority over a categorical demand.

Kant would be worried about the unchecked expansion of hypothetical imperatives into alleged duties, which people today do all the time—not to good effect. People become so preoccupied with their own goals and desires that they neglect the actual demands of morality, that is, the categorical imperatives.

As a consequence, people are less free because they're not meeting moral demands. Such people are weighed down by shoulds that cannot possibly be met, which may contribute to them feeling like moral failures. Furthermore, people lose the present moment because they are either looking backward with regret or forward to an imagined future.

A few examples will make it obvious how people get buried under a flood of shoulds in the form of hypothetical imperatives. Imagine that you love to ride your bicycle and live in a gorgeous place to ride. On a day of glorious weather, you say to yourself, "I should go out on a ride," even though you are exhausted or have other demands on your time. Either you go on the ride—but perhaps you are too cranky to enjoy it (even though you *should*)—or you ride and think to yourself, *But I really* should *be writing a piece on the power of should*; perhaps you don't ride at all and feel like a failure or lazy bones. Rather than appreciate what you are doing right now, you lose the present moment by imagining what you should have been doing.

Or imagine that you love to entertain and that you measure your self-esteem by how others regard you. You decide to have a dinner party, when you're suddenly buried in a shoulding avalanche. You *should* choose a main dish that is complicated and sophisticated. You *should* pair it with sides that will complement its flavors. The music *should* provide an ambience that will lead to deep, thoughtful, and engaging conversation. And of course, you *should* clean the house and even all the cupboards, because people might peek. In this case, you lose the pleasure you claim to love (entertaining). You might be the sort of person who only enjoys a feeling of satisfaction retroactively, once all your guests are gone.

Finally, imagine you are a perfectionist in recovery. Perfectionism is the ultimate form of the Should Storm, which makes it a form of self-deception. Everything becomes something you should not only do but do *perfectly*. You might say, "progress not perfection" in your twelve-step fellowship, but secretly you still subscribe to "perfection or bust." You should never have thoughts about drinking. You are the person who will wedge in the bicycle ride and the dinner party, sponsor people in your twelve-step group, sew your child's costume (well, actually, *all* the cast's costumes) for the school show, *and* write the grant to help the local pet shelter. You lose what you can do right now adequately or competently to an imaginary level of perfection.

Mistaking hypothetical imperatives for categorical imperatives can result in catastrophic failure. It's impossible to meet all the demands created by our goals and wants. Some of our demands will clash because the desires that spawned them clash—we are often not consistent in what we want. There are also practical constraints on what we are able to do. A person cannot write a grant and host a party at the same time; it just isn't going to happen. If she believes those practical constraints don't apply to her, then she suffers from terminal uniqueness and holds herself to standards that are impossible to meet.

People who are not governed but tyrannized by oughts and shoulds will judge themselves harshly, as inadequate, lazy, or failing. A person can also come to resent herself or parts of herself. She may also come to resent those who do not similarly acquit themselves of their obligations, resent others who acquit their obligations better than she does, and ultimately experience an anger that knows no bounds. This is what may keep you from meeting your genuine moral obligations.

People in recovery can be especially vulnerable to turning too many goals, desires, or considerations into categorical imperatives. This may be a consequence of feeling like one has to do a lot in order to make up for all the pain and suffering one caused oneself and others during one's using days. Overcompensation almost always misses the mark. Other instances of over-shoulding involve people with very good intentions trying to do too much. When even the best intentions outstrip practical considerations and limitations, the results can be disastrous.

Back to Stuart and Kant: If you want to avoid volcanoes of resentment and anger that produce very bad results, stop shoulding all over yourself. (This would count as a contemporary formulation of a counsel of prudence.) Learn to identify where shoulds properly belong in your life and where they have begun to colonize invasively.

Having said all this, what about the question of whether someone should stop using? What kind of imperative is involved in such a case? The answer depends on what the person is using and how that use affects her life. For illegal substances or behaviors, Kant would argue that one has a duty never to procure and engage in those substances and behaviors. Such an action (led by the maxim to use illegal drugs or substances whenever you want) involves breaking the law. If everyone broke the law, there really would no longer be a law. That's the contradiction.

Kant would also say that a person who uses illegal drugs is using herself merely as a means to an end to her enjoyment from an illegal activity. She is using herself much like she might use another person to get access to her drugs. Therefore, Kant would conclude, she has a duty to never use these drugs, so she should stop.

The harder cases are those involving legal substances and behaviors. Should a person who drinks occasionally, and never to bad effect, stop drinking? Kant might say there is a hypothetical imperative if drinking is related to some other goal or end. If a person drinks only lightly as part of work-related social gatherings, because not to do so might draw some scrutiny, then there is no reason he should stop. If that light drinker is partnered with someone newly in recovery and she wants to be supportive by acting in solidarity, then there is a should in the form of a hypothetical imperative.

How about the person who has moved down the spectrum of a substance use disorder such that many parts of her life are adversely affected by her use? Let's make this scenario even more complicated. She genuinely does not care what happens to herself. Her counsels of prudence have long since been extinguished. *Should* this person stop? Kant might argue this person has a duty to stop using. One part of his argument would be that the person is using herself to destroy herself. He would probably see a person drinking herself to death as a form of suicide, which is contrary to self-preservation. Kant argues that one has a duty not to commit suicide, which means that a person has a duty to stop using.

People who have progressed far down the spectrum of a substance use disorder are the ones who may have the hardest time seeing their duties and obligations. They are the opposite of people whose shoulding capacities are in overdrive, but the two groups share the same hindrance: neither is able to see the proper scope of their responsibilities. As such, neither is free. On the upside, this need not be a permanent state of affairs. People can learn to identify the imperatives that have a genuine and legitimate hold on them.

People who have progressed far into their addictions can learn from others who have been in similar straits but who are now able to meet their obligations and duties. Meeting even a small demand—perhaps the smallest hypothetical imperative she could generate for herself—may provide a much-needed boost. No success is too small when one feels like a failure. One success may also provide the groundwork for future attempts at success. Of course, there will be some failures. Some of those failures can be rectified; they provide valuable learning opportunities. With success we achieve the important recognition that we are the type of person who meets demands. As we meet hypothetical and moral imperatives, we become free.

Chapter Eleven

FEELING LIKE A MORAL FAILURE

Why is it so easy for some of us to feel like a moral failure, often about the most common and ordinary things? Anything can elicit this judgment. It may be liking the "wrong" kind of music or books; dieting and not keeping the weight off; having a medical condition; considering drinking after years of sobriety; or not being able to stop someone else from making bad choices. It is a harsh and debilitating judgment. Yet, for many, this feels true. Why do we do this to ourselves? And why do we do it so well? Whether in recovery or not, it is hard to avoid making this judgment.

Feeling like a moral failure has at least four sources: embarrassment, lack of self-trust, shame, and an inability to recognize the proper scope of responsibility each person has. Each of these can be a small step on the stairway to full-blown addiction, and being in recovery does not inoculate us against this condition.

Embarrassment is the feeling of being caught or exposed with something that makes you feel different from or inferior to others. There's often a strong undertow of guilt. A Shakespeare scholar who secretly devours romance novels may think that someone with her education really ought to have better taste. She doesn't, so she feels like a moral failure. A person who gets intoxicated at the office holiday party and makes inappropriate comments to his coworker may feel acute embarrassment the next day. Embarrassment is usually localized. One feels embarrassed about a particular action or type of action. Embarrassment tends to recede the further one gets away from the particular action or situation.

Gradually, a person stops trusting her knowledge, commitments, or abilities in one area of her life. The dieter who struggles to maintain her weight may not trust herself in certain food situations, while she is confident and secure in other areas of her life. But the one area where she isn't so trusting of herself becomes emblematic for what's wrong with her. She's convinced she's a moral failure. The same worker who got intoxicated at last year's holiday party, and then at the fiscal end-of-year party, may start to doubt himself around workplace parties. He knows he has made mistakes and embarrassed himself more than once, so he tells himself he won't have anything to drink this time.

Shame is a global attitude one has about oneself. The lack of self-trust spreads to more and more areas of one's life, mushrooming into a sense of unworthiness. The person with long-term recovery who begins to think about using when everything is going so well in life wonders what is wrong with him. A total loser like him doesn't deserve all that he has. He feels like a moral failure. The worker who moves from embarrassment to a lack of self-trust may progress to full-blown shame if he does not deliver on his own intentions not to drink and not to make inappropriate comments. When these comments eventually result in a situation where he is fired on the spot, loses a job he loves, and disappoints himself and his family, he may feel ashamed about the type of person he is. He has become the loser.

An inability to recognize the proper scope of responsibility is an important, but not fully recognized, cause of feeling like a moral failure. Either we don't take enough responsibility, or we take too much. Many of us did not take enough responsibility for our actions while in our active addictions. Instead of taking responsibility, we denied, minimized, or rationalized. If we did take responsibility, we were often ineffectual by either misplacing it or overcompensating with grand gestures and promises. If we made grand enough gestures, we thought it was enough to make up for all the ways that we had failed to meet our obligations. This dynamic along with the responsibility dodging techniques of denying, minimizing, and rationalizing are familiar, while cases where people take too much responsibility are less so.

Too many of us extend our responsibility in the wrong direction or to the wrong degree. We make some issues into moral matters where they are not. We also tend to assume responsibility for matters that are not ours. Three examples will demonstrate how responsibility guided in the wrong direction or to the wrong degree will make a person feel like she is a moral failure.

The first involves a person who has asthma that is well managed through medication, a strict exercise regimen, and prudent avoidance of triggers. There is nothing she could have done to prevent its development. Yet when the asthma flares up, she cannot help but think she should have been able to prevent it. Had she only done this or that, she would not be in this asthmatic distress. No amount of knowledge about asthma shakes her from her conviction. She thinks she is a moral failure.

The second example is a person who is unable to stop her friend from making a really bad decision. The decision leaves her friend in a world of pain. Let's imagine she did everything we might expect a best friend would do. She spoke to her friend in loving and compassionate ways. In a nonjudgmental way, she pointed out the pros and cons of different ways of proceeding. She enlisted others who also have the friend's best interest at heart. She supported her friend in a similar situation earlier. She did everything right, and it wasn't enough. She judges herself to be a moral failure.

The final example is a person married to an active alcoholic who believes she should be able to control the environment in such a way that her husband won't have reason to drink. She works full time to take some of the financial burden off her husband. She does most of the childcare and household work so he won't need to do it. She does everything to smooth out the rough edges in his life, yet her husband still drinks. She thinks, *If only I were better, I could keep him from drinking.* She views herself as a moral failure. What's the appropriate scope of responsibility in each of these cases?

The first step requires us to identify what is a moral matter or concern. The second involves identifying where a person's control begins and ends. The asthmatic transforms her medical condition into a moral condition. Allergies are not usually taken to be moral matters. Molds and pollens and one's physiological reactions to them generally fall outside the scope of things for which we expect people to take responsibility because they are caused by things well beyond their control. The asthmatic operates with the assumption that if something is in her control, she is responsible. The problem is that the asthmatic is wrong about what is and is not in her control. She believes she should have been able to at least control her reactions. This is impossible, yet she believes that she is responsible for doing so. Her inability to control what cannot be controlled and her failure to meet her responsibilities quickly lead her to conclude that she is a moral failure.

The case of the two friends involves a relationship, which is clearly a moral matter. The real issue is attempting to identify how far the responsibilities of each of the two friends extend and where they intersect or overlap. Here, too, it is necessary to identify what is in a person's control and what is not. The well-intentioned friend makes the huge leap of assuming that she is responsible for both the bad decision her friend makes and all of its consequences. It is impossible for the well-intentioned friend to control her friend's choices and the consequences of those choices, yet that is what she thinks she should do. The friend made her choice and bears responsibility for the consequences. A person who assumes she can and *must* do the impossible will always be in the position of feeling like a moral failure.

The case of the alcoholic husband and his wife is also a moral matter. The crucial dynamic is that she is attempting to control the environment and, by extension, the intentions that guide her husband's drinking. She's trying to remove all the reasons she believes her husband has to drink. The asthmatic, the well-intentioned friend, and the codependent wife all make different versions of the same mistake. By treating factors that are well beyond their control in the same manner as the ones within their control, each cultivates a misguided sense of responsibility. Each seriously misses the mark because she has assumed responsibilities that are not appropriately hers. There is a cruel irony here. People who are concerned with doing the right thing and meeting all their moral responsibilities are the most likely to feel like moral failures. Many will then try even harder, which creates even more opportunities to feel like a failure.

Being in recovery helps people identify what belongs in their realm of responsibility and what doesn't. They are encouraged to pay attention to their own side of the street. Embarrassment is not a bad thing in and of itself. It can be an important early warning signal that a person has done something that wasn't quite right or appropriate. It may keep a person from repeating the same mistake. And people who get over the embarrassment often become more self-aware. Embarrassment can be a learning opportunity and a good way to ascertain what matters to a person. Self-knowledge is always a good thing.

The dynamics of shame are trickier than embarrassment. In its earliest stages, shame can still play a positive role. When a person does something that makes her question her core values or how she sees herself, it prompts self-reflection. She may find herself asking, "Do I really want to be the type of person who does that?" Shame is opportunistic. It spreads quickly and may rapidly lose whatever possible benefits it carried. When shame envelopes the whole person, it is much harder to break free from it. Many recovery programs provide people the opportunity to examine a crucial source of their shame—their using. For many, using was the cause of their great shame and, probably for just as many others, shame about something else acted as an accelerant to their using. But when a person is able to identify the dynamics of shame in one area of her life, she is better equipped to do it in another.

Cultivating the ability to recognize the proper scope of one's responsibility is one of the most difficult tasks, whether one is in recovery or not. Some of us in recovery may always feel as though we have a lot to make up. We will assume more than our fair share in order to atone for our past failures. In our eyes, the scales may never rest evenly. In other cases, some obvious and deeply rooted gendered dynamics are in play. The example of the wife and her alcoholic husband was intentional. Societal expectations about being a good spouse and a good parent are much higher for women than for men. Women constantly judge themselves against a standard that can't be met. Knowing that the standard cannot be met may not be enough to keep a woman from judging herself against it. Feeling like a moral failure is almost a guarantee. This is why it is vital for women to be able to identify what is in their control and within the realm of their responsibility.

There are large gaps between *feeling* like a moral failure, *acting* in a way that morally fails, and *being* a moral failure. Feeling like a moral failure because one overextends one's responsibility is a form of self-deception; a person "gets it wrong" about what's hers and what is not. The constant feeling of being a moral failure is one of the most difficult dynamics a person can confront in herself.

Acting in a way that morally fails, or failing habitually, so that one consistently does not meet one's obligations calls for moral repair. Some situations can be repaired if the person is willing to do the difficult work. Repairing one's character is an onerous task. It is not impossible but requires a high degree of intention and commitment that can seem overwhelming. If we want to fundamentally alter our character for the better, there are no shortcuts. Halfhearted efforts only compound failures, which is why we should avoid them.

Chapter Twelve

THINKING AND LIVING CONTRADICTIONS

ACTIVE ADDICTS HAVE AN ABILITY TO EMBRACE AND LIVE CONTRADICTIONS. In formal logic, a contradiction has the form "p & ~p," where "p" is a variable and can stand for anything, and "~" means "not." For example: I am painting the bathroom today (p), and (&) I am not painting the bathroom today (~p). The door is open, and the door is not open. I am having an affair, and I am not having an affair. In other words, a contradiction is a statement that affirms and denies at the same time. It is impossible for a door to be open and not be open at the same time. The same is true for my painting the bathroom today. It is even true of my contradictory feelings about an affair: it is not possible, logically speaking, to have an affair and not have an affair at the same time. A contradiction is always false. Many addicts become habituated and adept at believing and living contradictions; it becomes a way of life. It explains why it can be so hard for nonaddicts to understand us.

Of course there is a big difference between the spotless world of logic where a statement is either true or false (no gray middle area exists) and everyday life. If the world of logic is a manicured lawn, the real world is an overgrown forest. We addicts traffic in messiness. Some of us thrive on it because we can hide in it.

What are some of the contradictions that active addicts live? For starters we may believe we can control our using while, at the exact same time, believing we cannot. We have plenty of evidence showing that we cannot control it, yet we remain firmly in the saddle of our belief that we can. We also believe that *this* will be the last time we drink, all the while inhabiting a sense of inevitability that we will use again. And, most obviously, many of us would say, "I knew I was an alcoholic, *but I knew I was not an alcoholic.*"

In his great dystopian novel, 1984, George Orwell introduces the concept of "doublethink." He defines it as the capacity to hold two opposing beliefs in mind at the same time, and to think of them both as true. Also, to consciously lie while sincerely believing in what one says; to ignore any truth that no longer serves one, but as soon as it becomes important again to recall it for just so long as it is useful. It requires one to negate objective reality while at the same time acknowledging the very truth one negates.[37]

All of this is indispensably necessary in living a life of active addiction, which involves attempting to manufacture reality. After all, who would want to accept a reality in which one is an addict and has lost one's self-respect as well as the respect of others? It seems easier to change one's perception of reality than it does to change one's behaviors, and hence, actual reality.

Denial and rationalization play huge roles in maintaining doublethink. They are first cousins. Denial is the ability to write off or rewrite what is happening. It involves minimizing. Rationalizations are really excuses that make one's actions acceptable. An alcoholic might say, "This binge was not as bad as the last one. I didn't black out." She denies the significance of a binge by comparing it to something more serious or dangerous. She ignores the inconvenient fact that binges are dangerous. If she does black out, she may rationalize it not as a consequence of drinking too much but rather being exhausted from working so many long hours. She becomes an expert at creatively rewriting her experiences.

We can also engage in doublethink when we make promises to ourselves and others that we will quit. William James, in *The Varieties of Religious Experience*, makes the keen observation that one cannot become a new person and still hold on to one's old ways. He captures the point beautifully.

> A drunkard, or a morphine or cocaine maniac, offers himself to be cured. He appeals to a doctor to wean him from his enemy, but he dares not face blank abstinence. The tyrannical drug is still an anchor to windward: he hides supplies of it among his clothing; arranges secretly to have it smuggled in in case of need.[38]

When a boat is anchored, it faces the wind. The anchor is dropped over the bow (windward), which stops the boat from blowing backward. Drugs are the anchor that keeps a person in the same place even as he says he is moving away from them.

What does it mean to offer oneself "to be cured?" What counts as a genuine offer or effort? Here is where doublethink can be especially dangerous. One can genuinely believe one is making one's best faith effort, but at the same time be lying to oneself.

Deliberately. Usually we think deliberate lies are told to others but we can do it to ourselves when the incentives or stakes are high enough. We have a vested interest in understanding ourselves and the world in certain ways. A deliberate lie is one way to manage and manipulate our own perception of reality. It can also be useful to manipulate others' perceptions of reality.

A deliberate lie is always intentional (as opposed to accidental) and always serves a purpose. Lies are more or less effective depending on how trustworthy a person is believed to be. The more trustworthy a person has been, or at least appeared to be, in the past, the greater the likelihood that the lie will be believed. The more trusting a person is, the more likely he is to believe a lie. So long as there is some level of trust, there's a good chance a lie will work. Distrust makes lies lose their power and efficacy. Caught enough times, a person loses his trustworthiness. However, doublethink works to preserve and manufacture new reserves of trustworthiness. The person who is most adept at doublethink will regard himself as most trustworthy.

The person who keeps some of the substances around (even, or especially, if hidden really well) and leaves open doors to past addictive behaviors is hedging his bets. This is a form of self-deception. He tells himself he is stopping but he is also telling himself that he isn't stopping. Doublethink also helps fuel the expansion of what counts as a "just in case moment" when he would use the substance or engage in the problematic behavior again.

Doublethink, with its accompanying lies, denial, and forgetting of "inconvenient fact," may also be directed toward others and adopted by them. Manufacturing your own reality can be exhausting; it may be easier to change the perceptions of those around you and enlist them in your manufactured reality. In other words, it's not just addicts who are capable of doublethink.

Enablers and codependents are often right there with us creating and maintaining an alternate reality.

A partner of an alcoholic may say things are getting better because instead of hard liquor her spouse now only drinks beer. Drinking beer instead of the usual whiskey is a form of weaning, she believes. She denies that the alcohol content and the calories of beer present serious health concerns. She'd rather buy the beer and keep plenty on hand than have him stop at the liquor store where he might be tempted to buy whiskey or stop at the local bar where he might also be buying rounds for his friends. When he comes home after a day at work ranting about his boss, it is tempting to rationalize his behavior. If only his boss would be more understanding or less demanding, he would not drink. If only his coworkers would do their fair share of the work, he would not drink. The list of "if onlys" can be quite long. When he comes home one day after work and is drunk, he may deliberately lie to her. Deliberate lies not only contribute to manufacturing an alternative reality, but they also disarm and neutralize another person's perspective. At their most insidious and effective, lies can make people around us feel crazy, disloyal, or morally blameworthy for challenging our perspectives on reality.

Doublethink creates a complete inversion of responsibility. An addict may see himself as having little or no responsibility for all that has led up to his active addiction and all that follows from it. If our enablers have long lists of "if onlys," the lists of addicts are limitless. Everyone and everything is more responsible for our addictions than we are. We make ourselves into victims of fate and circumstance and are unable to see how we were acting freely and taking ourselves down certain paths. To manipulate another's reality and to make her feel crazy in the process are deeply troubling actions for a host of reasons. Kant would say it constitutes disrespecting the humanity of another because we are using the other person as a means to our own end: to manufacture a reality that is more acceptable to us than the truth.[39]

Believing and acting based on doublethink become habitual. While some very intentional and deliberate actions may sometimes spring from it, eventually there will be many more that are unconscious and unintentional. The more we engage in doublethink, the more it is reinforced and the harder it is for us to recognize. This means that our self-deception runs ever deeper. Doublethink becomes our normal; we become more willing to embrace the contradictions than we are to reject them. In important ways, it is the very tension created by the competing claims that hold our reality together. Rejecting one of the competing claims is a terrifying prospect: our reality will be fundamentally altered because we would have to concede that only one of the options is true, real, or viable.

When we are so habituated to doublethink—manufacturing and manipulating so that appearances now masquerade as reality—we are in the depths of Plato's cave. We are in our chains, facing forward, unable to look in any other direction. At its worst, doublethink convinces us, or we convince ourselves, that not only is this how things *are*, but this is how things *must* be.

The "must" carries a lot of weight. Doublethink in the context of addiction strips away our fundamental agency—our ability to choose to act. As mentioned earlier, some of us made ourselves the victims of other people or circumstances. We handed over our agency to "these people" or "bad breaks" or "missed opportunities." It is they who caused us to become addicted, and our circumstance that pushed us over the edge. The more we see ourselves as victims, the more we understand ourselves as not having options or choices. We might tell ourselves that whatever we do, it doesn't matter. We no longer see ourselves as having free will, and that is one of the most debilitating effects of doublethink. Without free will we resign ourselves to fatalism about our addiction. Left unaddressed, addiction and fatalism can be life threatening, if not life destroying.

Chapter Thirteen

MORAL INDIFFERENCE

THE STATEMENT, "I DON'T CARE," HAS BECOME A COMMON REFRAIN to almost any sort of question. Where or what to eat, what to watch on television, or where to go on vacation may elicit this nonanswer. In many if not most of the cases, "I don't care," really means, "I don't have an opinion," with the companion plea of "you decide." "I don't care" can also mean, "I do not have an interest or investment in the question or situation." There is a whole host of situations where not caring is morally neutral. For example, I truly do not care whether the local baseball team makes the playoffs.

However, the "I don't care" response is expanding into more areas of life, especially where people *should* have a moral care, concern, or interest. When individuals genuinely do not care, the result can be moral apathy, moral callousness, and, finally, moral indifference. Apathy and callousness are stages on the way to indifference, which is one of the most dangerous and devastating orientations we can have in the world. The progression from apathy to indifference also describes the progression of addiction.

In its current usage, apathy is considered a lack of motivation to achieve certain goals. Someone who is apathetic may be taken as lazy or just disengaged when it comes to certain matters. A person can be apathetic about one set of goals or circumstances but quite dedicated to others. Sometimes the apathy in one area of life is masked by overconcern or diligent action in others. A person may believe because she is working so hard in *this* area, she is entitled not to do any work in *that* area.

Apathy tends to be localized and confined, but it can also seep into other areas of life. Acting apathetically can become a habit, Aristotle would say. One can progress from acting apathetically to being apathetic. Milder forms of substance use disorders, for example, can be both a cause and consequence of apathy. Many whose use becomes progressively worse tend to lose their motivations in more parts of their lives, which may in turn fuel their use.

Moral callousness is a kind of insensitivity to the cares, concerns, needs, or well-being of others. Callousness has a strong undertone of selfishness; one regularly puts one's self-interest ahead of the interests of others. Callousness becomes progressively worse. Kant argued all people have a duty to help some others, at some times.[40]

When the categories of "some others" and "some times" continue to shrink for a person, she becomes increasingly callous. She is less and less willing to act in ways that meet the needs of others, despite recognizing those needs. Moral callousness is often aided and abetted by rationalization, which helps a person reclassify or reprioritize the needs of others. Some needs may be written off as unimportant, while others are classified as being best or most appropriately met by others. In a more extreme form, a morally callous person will *blame* others for having needs or for being in circumstances that require the assistance of others.

Moral callousness can also be directed toward oneself. Internally directed callousness is especially debilitating because it is inescapable. Here, too, a person makes herself the measure of all things. She may so undervalue her own concerns and interests that she does not see herself as having equal moral standing to others. She might think to herself that her interests do not matter *because* they are hers. Or she may think herself weak or dependent or create some other harsh judgment for having needs and requiring the help of others. Since she is so weak or blameworthy for having needs, she may believe that she does not deserve the compassion, help, and friendship of others. She may be mired in shame, which provides a powerful reason to use. Her increased use will in turn become a bigger source of shame.

The person who is morally callous to herself becomes less capable of meeting a moral requirement Kant argues all humans have to improve oneself some of the time.[41] This is a companion duty to helping others some of the time. The person morally callous to herself will reduce the ways and times she does try to improve herself, perhaps seeing it as a waste of time (because of the kind of person she is) or as a self-indulgence that can never be justified satisfactorily for her.

Moral apathy and callousness each admit of degrees, which implies both bad news and good news. The bad news is that people can become increasingly apathetic and callous. The good news is that people can become less apathetic and callous. For a variety of reasons, one *can* become motivated to make positive changes; we see this all the time when someone stops using. We see it when someone has an experience that pierces the hardened shell that callousness creates. That one experience may create a crack that creates more cracks. Compassion can replace callousness, which may motivate a person to act in ways that tend to the care of others or herself.

Moral indifference, as opposed to mere apathy, belongs in its own category; it is the devastating combination of the worst forms of moral apathy and moral callousness. It does not admit of degrees, and this is what makes it so dangerous. Where a person becomes incapable of, or constitutionally unwilling to, cultivate moral emotions and to recognize the needs of others, she becomes morally indifferent. There is no motivation to help others (apathy), and there is an utter disregard for the interests and concerns of others (callousness). Nobel prize winner and Holocaust survivor Elie Wiesel famously said, "The opposite of love is not hate, it's indifference. The opposite of art is not ugliness, it's indifference. The opposite of faith is not heresy, it's indifference. And the opposite of life is not death, it's indifference."[42]

Moral indifference is a consequence of the complete absence or silencing of moral emotions. Without these moral sentiments, we have no motivation to act, according to philosopher David Hume (1724–1776). The entire basis of our moral systems and our ability to judge good from bad would crumble. Even if our reason were fully intact, reason alone is not sufficient. As Hume claimed: it isn't contrary to reason to prefer the destruction of the entire world to scratching one's finger. Choosing one's own total ruin is not contrary to reason.[43] If severe addiction is an instance of total ruin, then it is not contrary to reason to prefer it to recovery. So, what makes preferring the destruction of the entire world and choosing my own total ruin morally troubling? The answer is found in the right balance between one's emotions and one's reason.

Our palate of moral emotions seems to be shrinking and we pay scant attention to moral development. The emotions that are more other-regarding—putting one's concern for the welfare of others before one's own—are being supplanted by narrower and more self-interested emotions. When more and more people tend to understand themselves not to have an investment in the well-being of others and not to have obligations to others and self, it becomes easier to willfully ignore entire categories of others who have needs and legitimate expectations.

What does moral indifference to oneself look like? It's when in answer to the question, "Shall I live or shall I die?" the response is "I really don't care." This person does not have an investment in his own well-being. Moral indifference is a complete lack of care for one's soul, self, or person. It's as if a person had abdicated any agency and responsibility for living life. What is so disconcerting about a person who is truly indifferent toward herself is that she may be swayed neither by an appeal to reason nor by an appeal to emotions. All the virtues rooted in emotion and reason have no pull on her; she sees neither their agreeableness nor usefulness. She is unmoved. Her reasoning may be firing at full force, which makes it easy for her to dispatch any counterarguments others offer. Destruction of the entire world and scratching of one's finger are on par for her; so is active addiction and recovery. There's no argument sufficiently compelling to move a person one way or another when she really doesn't care about what happens to herself.

To the vast majority of people, the morally indifferent person is beyond the bounds of our comprehension; we cannot find our feet with him. We need to realize that all our arguments about the benefits of recovery rest upon value judgments about different ways of being in the world and ideas about a sufficiently high quality of living. Though a person may be beyond our comprehension, does that mean he is no longer capable of character rehabilitation or cure? Aristotle wrestled with this question. He was concerned that people who repeatedly and habitually engage in bad acts run the risk of becoming morally vicious persons. Moral viciousness is a character state; it is a chronic condition. The moral viciousness precludes the right kind of self- and other-love that is rooted in a care and concern for character.[44] In other words, it is a way of being in the world. For some, it is a form of life in the sense Wittgenstein discussed. The depravity itself can provide a morally depraved person with the framework for making sense of all her experiences.

For Aristotle, there is a balance between reason and emotion that gets (possibly permanently) ruined, in the morally vicious person. It seems obvious that his emotions have been affected, but Aristotle claims his reason is affected as well, which is different from David Hume's viewpoint. The morally vicious person's reason becomes defective in a way that means it no longer has dominion over the emotions. When a man reaches this point, Aristotle claims, he is no longer pardonable and no longer curable. Only if a man is able to retain some ability to care can he be cured.[45]

It all turns on the ability to care; yet moral indifference is the absence of care. There are people so far progressed in their addictions that they do not care; they are not capable of care. However, there are many severely addicted people who do not care because they feel as if they themselves and everything around them did not matter. Too much bad has happened, and too much has been lost. There's no meaning or value in caring. This is a severe existential concussion with potentially fatal consequences.

One cannot make another take care or have care. The best we can do is show through our own ways of living that it is still possible to find and make meaning.

Chapter Fourteen

WHAT YOU DO BECOMES
WHO YOU ARE

WHERE PHILOSOPHERS ONCE SPOKE OF CHARACTER AND MORAL VIRTUES, PSYCHOLOGISTS ARE more likely to speak of "personality types." The expression "moral character" has largely disappeared, which is unfortunate. The eclipse of moral language makes it harder to identify the moral virtues a person possesses and wants to possess. The language of character and virtue needs a renaissance. We need it; it is absolutely vital that we pay as much if not more attention to our moral development as we do our intellectual development.

Pairing rich moral language with discussions of addiction is a delicate matter. For centuries now, addiction has been considered a moral failing; addicts were those who simply lacked the willpower and moral fortitude to stop. We suffered from weakness of will. Either we were totally impetuous or we overrode what our reason told us to do. Addicts were thought of as weak-willed, lazy, selfish, and guilty of a host of other blameworthy traits.

With the medicalization of addiction and a shifting tide toward explaining it as a "brain disease," the moral disapprobation has lifted some, and discussions about responsibility have shifted. This is clearly a very good thing. But blame and responsibility are only two thin slices of moral philosophy. Character and virtue belong in the moral realm and can illuminate many previously neglected dimensions of addiction and recovery.

Aristotle undertook an examination of moral virtues, investigating how one becomes virtuous and how one comes to have a good moral character. No one, Aristotle claimed, is born naturally morally virtuous.[46] This means it is crucial to pay attention to the ways in which people develop virtues and their character. Character development is an important form of education. David Hume offers an Aristotelian account of virtue and focuses heavily on the social usefulness of them. Both Aristotle and Hume explore the moral dimensions of relationships between individuals and relationships of individuals to broader communities. A society as a whole and its members individually function or live much better when the virtues of benevolence and generosity flourish.

For Aristotle, moral virtues involve both reason and emotion, which are part of human nature. Reason has dominion over the emotions and influences the degree to which an emotion is experienced and then acted upon. Hume, on the other hand, boldly claims in *A Treatise of Human Nature* (1739) that "Reason is, and ought only to be the slave of the passions, and can never pretend to any other office than to serve and obey them."[47] Hume's claim is provocative. He walks it back some when he recognizes that reason plays a crucial advisory role in the shaping and directing of emotions. However, he adamantly maintains that reason alone can never motivate a person to act. Emotions provide the motivational oomph.

For both Aristotle and Hume, a virtuous act is the mean between the extremes of excess and deficiency. The virtuous act is the one guided by reason that hits the sweet spot of appropriate emotional response and action in both degree and direction. To see the interplay of reason and emotion, imagine you have a friend who has broken a promise to have lunch with you. What should you do? Your reason lets you weigh various considerations and analyze the circumstances around her missing lunch. Does she do this frequently? If she missed lunch because a child was sick, this may be a mitigating factor. It may be harsh and excessive to cut her out of your life completely. If she missed because a better offer came along and this isn't the first time she's done something like this, the deficient response would be to act as if nothing were wrong and her behavior were acceptable.

What is the sweet spot or the virtuous mean in a case like this? It may involve a kind of generosity in response. Give her the opportunity to explain. Listen charitably and don't assume you know what she's going to say in advance, and don't take everything she says in the worst possible way. State if you feel slighted or taken for granted. Ask her to call if she is going to miss so that you don't sit there fanning the flames of resentment.

Through cultivating moral virtues and practicing them, a person develops his good moral character. The man of character, Aristotle claims, uses his reason to assess what a situation requires and then, from this knowledge and the firmness of his character, chooses and does the virtuous action. Since he's habituated to taking these sorts of actions, he doesn't always need to engage in deliberation. It isn't that he acts without thought; he's just done a lot of the thinking and deliberation earlier. A person becomes who he is by what he does repeatedly and habitually. He develops a second nature; he more often and immediately responds with bravery, generosity, compassion, and loyalty.

Some people develop characters or second natures that have more vices than virtues. People who become habituated to respond in mean and petty ways become mean and petty people. People who never share and are tight-fisted become tightwads. Someone isn't a bad person because she did one bad thing. But a person who quite frequently cheats, for example, does become a cheater at some point. There's no definite point at which someone moves from sometimes cheating to being a cheater. But it does seem as if we can chart the progression of a person's cheating.

Everyone—but especially people who are actively addicted and people in recovery—ought to examine the relationship between their actions and their character. The challenge is that we may lack the willingness and ability to critically examine ourselves. Denial, rationalization, minimization, shoulding, taking too much responsibility, and engaging in doublethink—all powerful forms of self-deception—interfere with an honest and rigorous assessment of actions and character. For example, many people would redescribe their actions that might appear to be cheating as something else. Or, they may argue that while they did cheat, everyone else did too, so it doesn't really count as cheating. Or they may creatively rewrite what they've done so that they understand themselves not to have any real choice in the matter. All these rationalizations make it harder for such people to even briefly consider that they are cheaters.

Ask most people to make a list of virtues and you'll likely be greeted by some blank looks and, eventually, some very short lists. What we need is a robust list of virtues so that we have even the possibility of undertaking an assessment of our character. Thankfully, David Hume gives us plenty of virtues in his *An Enquiry Concerning the Principles of Morals* (1751). Hume was a keen observer of human nature and activity. He believed that part of our nature is to have a spark of fellow feeling toward others and that this sentiment is the basis for morality. According to Hume, all humans share a similar psychological makeup, so it is not surprising that there seem to be some universal sentiments such as sympathy and benevolence.[48]

Every virtue, Hume claims, is greeted by our approval because it is pleasant and has a kind of usefulness, or what he calls "utility." The vices are met with disapproval because they cause or elicit a reaction of pain. Based on his observations, Hume creates four categories of moral virtues:

1. Virtues that are useful to self

2. Virtues that are immediately agreeable to self

3. Virtues that are useful to others

4. Virtues that are immediately agreeable to others

These categories and instances can be seen in this chart:

	SELF	OTHERS
Useful	Discretion, industry, frugality, caution, strength of mind, wisdom, memory, enterprise, assiduity, good sense, discernment, temperance, patience, constancy, perseverance, forethought, judgment, considerateness, peace of mind[49]	Benevolence, justice, gratitude, friendliness, truthfulness, fidelity, honor, allegiance, chastity, charity, affability, moderation[50]
Immediately agreeable	Cheerfulness, greatness of mind, courage, humility, dignity, tranquility, poetic talent, serenity, refined taste[51]	Good manners, wit, ingenuity, eloquence, affability, modesty, decency, politeness, gentility, cleanliness[52]

Two admissions: The first is that some of this language is unfamiliar; some of these words have largely disappeared from our common vocabulary. We've let some good concepts wither away from lack of use. Second, some of these virtues have gender, class, and racial dynamics. Hume is quite clear that chastity and modesty, for example, are more important virtues for women than men. Rather than reject Hume for this, one might instead take this as an opportunity to explore which virtues seem to have retained these gender, race, and class dimensions and why this is so.

Regardless of the path one chooses to make or take in recovery, it is vital that people be able to make an honest assessment of how they show up in the world and who they are. In the absence of such an assessment, one runs the risk of being self-deceived in some very significant ways. Self-deception can lead us to act in ways that are not in our best interest and that contradict our core moral values and principles.

Twelve-step programs suggest (since there are no requirements) that each person engage in an exhaustive and honest moral self-assessment. Step Four is to "Make a searching and fearless moral inventory of ourselves," while Step Five has us admit to "God, ourselves, and another person the exact nature of our wrongs."[53] These steps often strike terror into the hearts of newly recovering people. The assumption of many people is that Step Four requires a list of all our moral failings and Step Five involves the confession of those failings. The expectation is that by admitting our failings in this way, we take them out of the dark and give them a good airing out. Exposed to light and air, these wrongs lose some of their power over us. Failings, secrets, and shame can all be debilitating and can break people. Once they lose their power over us, we may be freer to make different choices and try to become different people.

But Steps Four and Five can also be disorienting to the point of debilitation. Unsurprisingly, people are often "stuck" on these steps for a long time. What had been familiar and even comfortable is now up for grabs. This is reminiscent of René Descartes, who was utterly vexed by the ways systems of knowledge failed to have an unshakeable foundation. In the hope of locating a foundation that would escape all doubt, Descartes in *Meditations on First Philosophy* undertakes a rigorous and, by his estimation, exhaustive inventory of all his beliefs about everything. In his *Meditation II*, Descartes writes that, "It is as if I had suddenly fallen into a deep whirlpool; I am so tossed about that I can neither touch down bottom with my foot, nor swim up to the top."[54] This is a very familiar feeling to many addicts. You can't sink far enough to push off to get back to the surface and yet you can't keep treading water. What can a person do in a situation like this? What can function as a moral life preserver?

This is where Step Four becomes crucial. A searching and fearless moral inventory must be just that. Our shortcomings, failures, and transgressions are not the entirety of our inventory. They may seem the weightiest but no person's moral inventory is simply failings and shortcomings. Step Four doesn't just look back at all the wrongs we have done and harms we have caused. It also looks at the present: what sort of good character traits, virtues, moral commitments, and concerns do we have? It can also look to the future: what sort of traits and commitments do I have that I can build on, and what traits do I want to cultivate?

As strange as it may sound, it may be easier for some of us to focus on our failures and defects. Some of these defects may have been part of the reason we started to use. Other defects may have developed right alongside our addictions. Many addicts tend to reserve the harshest judgments for themselves; it becomes a habit. The harshness of such judgments may be well-deserved. We tend to think that failings are proof of our bad moral character. We may have acted squirrelly and weaselly in the past; now we *are* squirrels and weasels. These failings are familiar to us, and familiarity provides a kind of comfort and a ready excuse not to do the hard moral work of improving one's character.

The sort of moral examination crucial to good recovery is akin to a massive home remodeling project. Descartes saw himself as a one-man demolition crew going to work on his house of knowledge. He wrote in *Discourse on Method*, "Now just as it is not enough, before beginning to rebuild the house where one lives, to pull it down, to make provisions for materials and architects, or to take a try at architecture for oneself, and also to have carefully worked out the floor plan; one must provide for something else in addition, namely where one can be conveniently sheltered while working on the other building."[55] Descartes's suggestions are spot-on for undergoing a moral renovation of your character and life.

A person who just tears herself down all the time really is neither interested in nor capable of moral renovation. This is where Step Four is important. Step Four is an assessment of the entire house: what parts present serious structural challenges or dangers even? What parts can be saved? If one does not make a complete assessment and instead focuses only on the negative, one may well demolish the good features along with the less desirable ones, because those will not be recognized. Throwing a Molotov cocktail is one way to engage in demolition but it tends not to leave much standing.

Steps Four and Five are the demolition work done in a prudent and careful way. One may need to knock down a load-bearing wall that is no longer up to the task, but then something else must carry that weight. Remove rotted sills. Do all of this while keeping an eye on Step Four. Demolition is a means to an end of home improvement; it doesn't leave one with nothing. Rather, it leaves the salvageable and good materials available for use in rebuilding.

Who is the architect overseeing this moral home renovation? One can employ an architect or try one's own hand. Many active addicts and people new in recovery may not yet be up to the task of being their own solo architect. In some ways they lack the experience, that is, the positive experience of being in the world sober. They may need to lean heavily on the advice and guidance of friends or whoever is hearing their Fifth Step. While they may not yet be ready to design an entire home renovation, they can begin to recognize what design elements work for them and which don't. This recognition is a huge achievement.

Descartes provides a crucial reminder that we need to live somewhere during the renovation process. We may need to "moral couch surf" for a while. And yet, a thorough and searching moral inventory that recognizes positive features also provides us with some shelter enabling us to do the hard work of rebuilding our moral selves. Rebuilding our moral selves requires imagination and vision directed in the right ways. It's a skill that people new in recovery may not have. It isn't that we lack imagination. On the contrary, many of us were very good at imagining worst-case scenarios, slights and hurts, and what we might do if only other people weren't standing in our way. Many are afraid to imagine a better self or a better future; it seems to invite trouble. A fear of imagination keeps people locked into a way of seeing themselves and the world. Being able to imagine things differently is crucial for recognizing possibilities and opportunities. Imagination expands the world, which is often frightening at the same time as it liberates.

Rich and robust moral language is crucial for imagining ourselves differently. Virtues link imagination and action together so we can become different types of people. If we could, for example, imagine ourselves as trustworthy and do some trustworthy deeds, we may act ourselves into becoming trustworthy people.

Chapter Fifteen

THE IMPORTANCE OF FRIENDSHIP

ARISTOTLE IS THE FIRST PHILOSOPHER TO OFFER CATEGORIES OF FRIENDSHIP. He does it in the context of trying to identify what sort of friendship is necessary for living the happiest and most virtuous life. Aristotle wants to demonstrate that the right kind of friendship is the most important relationship one person can have with another. This relationship trumps both marriage and parenting, which may seem heretical to married people or people with children. So important is friendship that "no one would choose to live without friends even if he had all others goods."[56] Without the right kind of friendship, one cannot live the best possible life.

Aristotle enumerates three types of friendship that differ from one another based on what each person likes about the relationship or wishes to gain in the relationship: pleasure friendship, utility friendship, and virtue or complete friendship.[57] Aristotle's language may seem a little foreign to us, but the distinctions he draws will be familiar. He would agree that many friendships are situational; they are products of the circumstances in which one finds oneself. The first two kinds—pleasure and utility—are both quite common and can be understood as involving people who are friends for a reason or friends for a season. The third type—virtue or complete friendship—is very rare and it is the one that contributes most profoundly to a person's happiness.

Pleasure friendship is based on the enjoyment that each person experiences in the relationship. Each person likes the pleasure or fun she experiences. This kind of friendship can be instantaneous. One can walk into a social gathering and see a person across the room who just looks like she is having fun. Or is fun. We can be drawn to that fun and want to participate. We may not see this person in other settings. This person may be the other parent who has been sitting with you during seasons of junior hockey. She's witty, kind, and smart. She's smart enough to bring an extra blanket for those long days of sitting on a metal bench in a hockey arena.

Aristotle says that the young tend to favor these sorts of friendships. They incline toward having fun and feeling good because they are governed more by their feelings. There may be something accurate about this, but as we get older most of us develop a better sense of what pleases us. We can be a little more intentional in striking up these sorts of friendships and appreciating the pleasure and good feelings they bring us. Pleasures can be fleeting and fickle though. As quickly as a pleasure friendship can be formed, it can be dissolved, according to Aristotle. Here, too, he is making reference to the fact that what young people find pleasurable can change quickly.

A utility friendship is based on the usefulness or benefit that each person experiences in the relationship. Each person likes the benefit he derives from the friendship. It may sound like a relationship where two people use each other, and there may be an element of truth in that. However, a utility friendship is often a matter of a shared situation and a shared need. Two employees who might not otherwise have much interest in each other may find themselves working together because they possess complementary skills. But needs can change quickly. Needs can also be met, fulfilled, and so no longer hold, in which case the basis for the relationship changes. When this happens, the utility friendship may dissolve.

Pleasure and utility friendships are incomplete, according to Aristotle. They are incomplete in part because their focus is on what each person "gets" from the other. Putting it in the least charitable way, each person likes the friend or the relationship because of how it makes her feel (some sort of pleasure) or how it meets her needs or wants (some utility). It isn't that there isn't goodwill for the other person; there must be some reciprocal goodwill for the relationship to be a friendship. But the goodwill is limited in how far it goes. It might not extend beyond the confines of the particular reasons or seasons for which one befriends another.

Pleasure and utility friendships are not bad. They play important roles in all of our lives. All is well so long as each person has the same set of expectations for the relationship. Trouble may ensue when one person understands the relationship to be deeper or more serious than the other. When one person derives too much benefit at the expense of the other, this may also be a problem. Goodwill can devolve into resentment when expectations change or are unmet.

If you ask addicted people about their friends when they were using, some common refrains emerge. As addictions progressed, people cut ties with friends. Long-term friends who predated our increasingly heavy use present a threat to us; they know us and what we used to be like. When we look into the eyes of people who knew us so well, we often recoil. We see what we used to be like. We might look at them and see what our life *could have been*. However, we have a heavy investment in convincing ourselves that we are fine, happy, or successful now. It is much easier to demonize another, especially when they express concern for us, than it is to allow even a brief glimmer of recognition that there may be some truth to what they're saying. As addictions further progressed, using became the basis for friendships. There may have been some pleasure. Some people who party really hard are fun. Often there is more than an element of utility; some of us used others who were able to make it easier or cheaper to get our drug of choice.

Pleasure and utility friendships that center on using are quite transient. As some of us recognized, we "drank or used down." We wanted to drink or use with people who did it more or worse than we did. That way, we would always have others with whom to favorably compare ourselves. We could convince ourselves that our use wasn't so bad because of what our friends were doing. But then came the time when we became part of the "drinking down" pool and provided the favorable comparison for someone else. For many people, especially when using, there is pleasure in making a favorable comparison of oneself against others. This also provides utility; we use other people in our denials and rationalizations.

Aristotle sets the bar very high for complete or virtue friendships. This type of friendship makes the most important contribution to a happy and virtuous life. Happiness and virtue are inseparable for Aristotle in a way that may puzzle contemporary readers. But he is making two simple and perhaps obvious points. First, we become who we are by what we do. Doing good, virtuous acts makes us have a character that appreciates the relationship between doing good things and being happy. The second point is that we do many things with our friends. The right friends uplift us, making us into better people. The wrong friends will be along for the ride that may end in a disastrous crash.

To be capable of virtue friendship, a person must first know herself and her character. She must also learn to identify other people who possess the right sort of character. This takes a certain amount of maturity and wisdom, which is part of the reason Aristotle would say that the young are not yet capable of having complete friends. As odd as it may sound, we need to learn how to be friends. It isn't something that we intuitively know, but rather can only learn through experience.

The person who is capable of virtue friendship has the right sort of care and concern for his moral character. Aristotle describes the self-love a virtuous person has as love of and for his virtues and character. He loves generosity, benevolence, bravery, loyalty, and trustworthiness. He acts in ways that spread these. He doesn't love them as possessions; one cannot hoard virtues. The virtuous man cherishes his character and does what he can to become an even more virtuous person. This may sound self-absorbed, but for Aristotle it is quite the opposite. For Aristotle, self-love and virtue friendship are connected. The man of character loves himself in such a way that he is his own best friend.

One way for a virtuous man to tend his character is to cultivate friendships with others who also tend to their character in this way. The person of good character loves his virtue friend for the *kind of person he is* and not for what he can get from that person. This is what makes the friendship complete.

Friendships based on virtue are rare. They require intention, careful cultivation, and hard work over a significant period of time, which means one cannot have many virtue friends. Intention, attention, diligence, and care are not the hallmarks of people active in their addictions. Friendship is an activity, not an emotion or disposition. Weeping or making grand drunken gestures about how great your friends are doesn't count.

Friends of the right sort provide moral mirrors to each other. No two people are identical in their moral virtues, and we often are drawn to people who have traits we'd like to emulate. They have something we want. We can also and must remain willing to see ourselves in the eyes of the other. A good friend can cut right through our layers of self-deception. When that person raises a concern to us about what we are doing, it carries some weight. It should make us sit up and take notice because we believe that person always has our best interests at heart. This is not to say that our friends are always right about us, but it is to acknowledge that our friends know us in certain ways that cannot be easily dismissed. We don't cut and run as we did when we were active in our addictions.

When we are most active in our addictions, we are not concerned with our character, which means it is impossible for us to be concerned about the well-being of others. Nor are we usually concerned in the right way for our own character. This can be devastating, Aristotle would say, because it may contribute to our becoming incapable of having and acting upon the right kind of concern. Active addicts are (temporally) not capable of the highest form of friendship.

Family members and friends often wrestle with the question of when to end a relationship or friendship with a person active in his addiction; it is one of the most gut-wrenching questions. Caught between desires to save our friend, to have things return to "normal," and waves of denial, a person often hangs in there for longer than is good for her and for the active addict. Staying in a friendship with someone who demonstrates a consistent lack of care and concern for herself and others can be harmful. If our care for her starts to overwhelm the care for our own selves, this is a serious problem.

People new to recovery often struggle with friendships. Should they cut ties with people who are still using? Our friends, while they're using, may not be the right fit for us. These friends may be only too happy to have us back using in their company down in Plato's cave. While we may recognize that some people pose special risks or hazards to us, it is never easy to just cut ties. This is an incredibly difficult struggle early in recovery and we are often unprepared for the grief and sense of loss we may experience even when we know it is the right thing to do. We then confront the problem of when and how to sever those ties. The learning curve for people new in recovery is painful and steep, especially when it comes to friends.

Getting into recovery provides one of the best and most effective ways of repairing the damage that has been done to one's character. Of course, a person in recovery must be the one to do the painful and difficult work, but she can do so in the company of others who share concerns for her character and well-being. In recovery, people do develop the kinds of friendships described by Aristotle. Pleasure and utility friendships play important roles, but if we develop a virtue friendship in the course of our recovery, we reap one of life's greatest rewards.

Chapter Sixteen

SUPERSIZING TO A PASSIONATE COMMITMENT

WE ORIENT OUR LIVES AROUND PEOPLE, PROJECTS, INTERESTS, AND CONCERNS that matter deeply to us. Some might argue this is what makes humans unique: we have the ability to set goals and then decide the best ways of achieving them. We orient our lives around our commitments—they become the axis around which life turns. An axis is an imaginary line that a body turns around. The earth revolves around its axis during a twenty-four hour period. In other words, an axis holds a body in place even as it revolves. Just as importantly, the axis is fixed and immobile because of the movement around it. An axis always involves a relationship, which is crucial for understanding how certain practices or commitments come to function as an axis for people.

In many ways we *choose* what will play the role of an axis in our lives. Parents often say it is their children. Others will say it is a spouse or partner. Some will say it is a career. Yet others will want to make the world a better place by fighting against various forms of discrimination or working to create more justice. We often think about the way living positive commitments makes us who we are or pushes us to be better people. A commitment is a set of promises that aims toward a certain goal or end. The crucial thing about commitments is that they can only be fulfilled by actions. Actions do speak louder than words. Words alone are merely ornamental.

The healthiness and the moral worth of a commitment may be tied to the duration, intensity, and means by which it is pursued. For example, a commitment to living a well-balanced life is generally seen to be a good thing. To embody this commitment is to engage in acts steadily and consistently. The right balance has to be struck over an extended course of time. A person isn't living a well-balanced life if she vacillates between all work and no enjoyment for months on end and then all enjoyment and no work on end. While there may be a type of balance (sixty days for one and sixty days for another), this balance is more illusory than actual. The content of the commitment matters enormously, too. A commitment to amass a fortune by any means no matter the cost to others is morally suspect. Imagine one then revises that commitment to "amass a fortune by any means no matter the cost to others so that I can give it all to a charity." Even with the added commitment to give it all way, the content is still troubling, as are the means to realize the goal.

Commitments are dynamic because they always need to be embodied in action. Commitments can change over the course of their duration to good or bad effect. A healthy set of commitments can become unhealthy when pursued to the wrong degree or by the wrong means. The person who is concerned to lead a well-balanced life may become so consumed with his own well-being that he begins to care less about the well-being of others. Unhealthy commitments or negative commitments can come to function as an axis, too.

Commitments can develop intentionally, while just as many develop unintentionally through habit or custom. A lack of attention or intention can produce commitments that a person may not even realize she is living. This is one way to understand addiction. Addiction is a supersized set of lived commitments. Using substances or engaging in certain behaviors becomes the axis around which an addict's life turns.

Addiction seems to sneak up on a lot of people. No doubt there are those who are just off to the races and develop a full-blown addiction swiftly. But there are a huge number of people who used or engaged in behaviors "normally" (contentious term) but then underwent some sort of shift. The shift may be physiological and related to tolerance, cravings, and withdrawal symptoms. This seems to be the experience of many people who use medications as medically prescribed. In some ways, they do everything "right" by following their doctors' orders, yet they end up physically dependent and addicted.

As addiction progresses, our use becomes the axis around which the vast majority of our relationships and activities will turn. It isn't accurate to say all things, because there are many people who are still able to function very effectively in some parts of their lives, all the while being full-blown addicts.

People moving down the continuum of a substance use disorder will discard relationships with people who challenge them on their use or who don't use in the ways they do. People will discontinue activities that would disrupt or interfere with their use. Such activities and relationships will become more peripheral and removed from the pull of the axis. They will eventually fall away, so that what remains are only the using activities and relationships that revolve around the axis. In turn, these using activities and relationships will hold the axis immobile.

With addiction, there is a high degree of homogeneity between the axis and the activities and relationships that revolve around it. Change or difference is something to be avoided, and so we addicts tend to seek the same things over and over again.

By holding so much of our lives in place, the axis creates stability. Many people crave stability over the uncertain and the unknown, and this is especially true for many addicts; we know our addictions. We know what life is like using. We don't know what life would be like not using. So, even though there are many downsides (to put it so very mildly) to addiction, the known will trump the unknown. Perhaps with an air of defiance, but more likely resignation, some people will argue that they're choosing the devil they know.

Commitments tend to scare active addicts; they are seen as confining or dangerous in a certain way. They're confining because they might require that we no longer do something we believe we should still get to do or that we can handle doing. Commitments invite scrutiny and accountability as well. For all the times we may have promised someone to stop using and yet did not, we are confronted with the statement, "You promised." It may be said in anger or resignation. It may be said as an accusation. Regardless of the delivery, it is the truth and the truth hurts.

Commitments may also seem dangerous because they hold the potential for failure. We may say that we are committed to certain things, but our actions are not congruent with our words. Not fulfilling commitments can actually reinforce our belief that we are incapable of doing so. And if we are the type of people who can't keep promises and fulfill commitments, why even bother to try?

Commitments orient a person in the world in part because they orient a person within herself. Our commitments act as a compass. In the absence of commitments, we career through life. William James describes people who are not centered or steady as having a life "whose existence is little more than a series of zigzags, as now one tendency and now another gets the upper hand. Their spirit wars with their flesh, they wish for incompatibles, wayward impulses interrupt their most deliberate plans, and their lives are one long drama of repentance and of effort to repair misdemeanors and mistakes."[58] This is perhaps one of the best descriptions that can be applied to active addicts; our lives are riddled with inconsistencies and contradictions. These are the very things that preclude commitments and make us unable to navigate our own lives at times. We are unable to get our bearings.

But people *do* change the most fundamental commitments in their lives. The axis metaphor is helpful here: Many people who get into recovery do so as a consequence of experiencing too much misery. The pain of a certain behavior or lifestyle is just too much, so something has to change. Some people will slowly discard their using behaviors or using friends. They will break off old pieces of their activities and relationships and replace them with new ones. By introducing new activities and commitments, the homogeneity of the axis and what holds it immobile is considerably weakened. This creates the possibility of a new set of commitments coming to function as an axis.

Other people experience a sudden and perhaps violent destruction of an axis. It is as if the axis were just ripped out of a person's life. A catastrophic loss, terrible tragedy, the body's breakdown, or some legal and financial problems may leave a person feeling as if the world were falling apart around her. In some ways, it is. The very thing that keeps a person oriented in the world and keeps her world ordered has been shattered. When an axis is destroyed, everything it was holding in place suddenly crashes down on the person, causing her to suffer an existential concussion.

People who suffer this sort of destruction of an axis have an opportunity that comes wrapped in a great challenge. Something needs to function as an axis. Without an axis, life has little order or meaning. Some will continue to use in part because their ability to imagine living differently and making different choices has been so damaged. The craving for stability in whatever form, no matter the cost, may keep a person using.

Others in the same position will choose to make recovery the axis around which life turns. Here the process of identifying and delivering on commitments is starting close to ground zero. Everything is up for grabs. In this case, people have the opportunity to more intentionally orient their lives. The opportunity may have been unwanted, but here it is nevertheless.

The commitment to recovery involves fundamentally altering how an addict *is* in the world. This cannot be done wholesale but only incrementally. Another crucial thing about promises and commitments is that one has to learn how to keep them. These are skills and require practice in much the same way as playing a musical instrument does. Never underestimate the importance of practice and habit.

As important as practice is, however, it is not sufficient by itself. Attitude matters; at some point, there needs to be passion. One needs to make a passionate commitment to a way of life. This is the change that happens when one moves from a commitment not to use to a commitment to live in recovery because one wants to be a different kind of person. The passionate commitment to a life of recovery is liberating. The long drama of repair and repentance is rewritten. Options that were foreclosed in our using days are reopened. New opportunities become available. Our actions and attitudes undergo a huge transformation.

Such a huge transformation means that we are regenerated, as William James would say. We are different people; we have liberated ourselves by living a passionate commitment. Consider what Wittgenstein says about religious belief and apply it in the context of a recovery program:

> It strikes me that a religious belief could only be something like a passionate commitment to a system of reference. Hence, although it's *belief*, it's really a way of living, or a way of assessing life. It's passionately seizing hold of *this* interpretation. Instruction in a religious faith, therefore would have to take the form of a portrayal, a description of that system of reference, while at the same time being an appeal to conscience. And this combination would have to result in the pupil himself, of his own accord, passionately taking hold of the system of reference. It would be as though someone were first to let me see the hopelessness of my situation and then show me the means of rescue until, of my own accord, or not at any rate led to it by my *instructor*, I ran to it and grasped it.[59]

Living in recovery is living with passionate commitment. It is an ongoing commitment to caring for your person and character. It is living in ways that make you be the kind of person you want to be. Passionately committing to recovery is grabbing hold of everything you have done and are doing, while at the same time opening your hands to reach for the future.

Chapter Seventeen

THE LIFE OF PLEASURE OR THE LIFE OF ETHICS

THE DANISH PHILOSOPHER, SØREN KIERKEGAARD, WROTE MANY WORKS OVER THE course of his relatively short life. He used various pen names that often had significance to his philosophical works. At other times he wrote as himself. Sometimes he would review his own works written under pseudonyms as "Søren Kierkegaard" or vice versa. He was also known to incite controversy between "Søren Kierkegaard" and these other "authors." While this may strike some as inappropriate or out-of-bounds, philosophers today are glad he did this because those "disputes" are very philosophically interesting. Of course in our Internet age, such maneuvers would be quickly detected and broadcast to the world.

Kierkegaard is rightly regarded as the father of existentialism, a philosophical approach centering on the individual and the freedom and responsibility she has in determining the course of her life. Kierkegaard frames responsibility in terms of the absolute responsibility for a person's relationship to God. The talk of God may be off-putting to some, but his discussions of anxiety, dread, and despair will be familiar to anyone struggling with addiction. It may seem counterintuitive, but despair and dread may be necessary steps on the way to a life of happiness.

As a Dane, Kierkegaard was raised in the state religion of Lutheranism. He had a contentious relationship with the Church. He did not question the existence of God, but he certainly questioned the notion of Christianity and its relation to or assumptions about faith. Part of Kierkegaard's concern was that faith was less a matter of an individual's core beliefs and more a matter of custom and habit. It is pretty easy to identify as a Christian when one is born into a family living in a culture with a state religion. Going to services is just what you do every Sunday. People sit in the same pew, sing the same hymns, and treat faith as something they express for that hour or two every Sunday. One's faith in this sense almost feels like something inherited, much like a watch from a grandfather or a well-worn coat from a grandmother. If you can put it on, you can just as easily take it off. To Kierkegaard, this seemed a very superficial account of faith. The exercise of faith becomes rote and formulaic; an individual gets on a preset track and moves along.

Kierkegaard's description of this "faith" is familiar to the many people who have lived it. When asked about their religious beliefs, many will answer that they were raised in a particular faith tradition but no longer practice or believe. They experience a divorce between their spirituality and religion. Religions, for many, are seen more as institutions, organizations, and even corporations. They are viewed as groups of people for sure, united by sets of beliefs about God, Allah, Yahweh, and sacred texts. Think about the ways the

"Catholic Church" is often assumed to be just the Vatican and/or other church officials and priests. What about the parishioners, the people who identify as Catholic? In general, individuals are seen as Catholic, but not as the Catholic Church. Kierkegaard might say that individual people can have faith, but a collection of these people does not have faith. The bottom line for Kierkegaard is that faith is a matter of the personal relationship that each person has with God. Faith is intensely personal; it concerns a one-on-one relationship. An individual bears sole—and the ultimate—responsibility for her own spiritual life.

Faith, according to Kierkegaard, is an existential stage of life. Having faith or leading a life of faith is not easy. Rather, it is an achievement won only through great anxiety and despair. One may need to pass through other existential stages in order to reach a state of faith. Faith is the highest existential stage and, once achieved, the other two will be incorporated into one's life. Addicts may find comfort in this description of existential stages, and see something of their own life trajectories in them.

The first existential stage Kierkegaard calls the "aesthetic." In philosophy, "aesthetic" means something concerned with art or beauty, or more specifically, the value of art and beauty. Something beautiful can bring pleasure, such as seeing the sunset across a vista or hearing a concerto performed flawlessly. Kierkegaard's usage is a little more down-to-earth, in a manner of speaking. Someone who lives an aesthetic life is deeply concerned with pleasures of all sorts; immediate gratification of them is the goal. Boredom is the sworn enemy since it means dullness. The aesthete wants intensity, passion, and vibrancy. The pursuit of pleasure is the orienting force in one's life. A person will weight activities that bring pleasure far more than those that do not. She also chases possibility at the expense of actuality. Like the person who keeps changing the channel on the television in search of a better show, even when she is watching one she likes, the aesthetic is always oriented to the possibility that something better is around the corner. Why wait when you can run to it?

The aesthete may have many friends and acquaintances. She may have something going on every day. She may be or is really happy; she may feel as if she has life by the tail. People are drawn to the aesthete because she glows so brightly. People want to be her or be like her. She is charismatic and a born leader. She is a pied piper who seems to walk lightly through the world.

Kierkegaard describes the aesthete as having feet formed so as not to leave footprints. Footprints require contact with the ground; they are the proof that shows someone has been somewhere and done something. Just like Peter Pan, the aesthete is not fully tethered to the world. She is light and airy, and does not engage in the sort of hard commitments that leave marks or traces. Rather than grapple with a tricky situation, she might choose to drift away, because a sustained engagement requires a commitment to work through a problem. [60]

For someone just starting to use substances, the life of the aesthete is very attractive. So many people say, "I use alcohol or drugs just to relax and loosen up so that I can fit in. I feel more comfortable, smarter, or funnier when I've got a good glow." We want that glow and rush. There is nothing like that first rush. We will continue to try to match it, even as we know it is impossible. Those first highs make everything seem more fun and intense. Our senses are heightened, and we feel as if we had never been better. We feel wittier and cleverer, like we are finally being the person we were always meant to be. Brain science is now demonstrating what we've already known: certain substances really do light up our pleasure circuitry; they trip the light fantastic like nothing else.

We like to surround ourselves with people who are vibrantly alive. Some of us want to be the center of the party while others are happy just being in the presence of those who burn so brightly. Drinking and drugging can be a lot of fun at first and may be for a good long while. It does no good to deny that. But for many of us, in seeking that rush or those great times, we require more and more of our substance of choice. Perhaps the fun starts to wane or comes at a cost, if small at first. We may well be ready to pay that price. As the price increases, however, we renegotiate and perhaps reset our expectations of what counts as "fun." Fun must always include alcohol and drugs.

Kierkegaard's second existential stage is the ethical one. Here, moral norms and values are the ties that bind. The focus is on realizing the universal moral norms or principles in all of our affairs. Some philosophers and psychologists have talked about stages of moral development and that, as one morally matures, one is guided by universal principles and norms. A morally mature person is able to separate out personal connections or preferences, and act in impartial ways. Kierkegaard regularly invokes the notion of the universal: there are demands or duties that hold on all of us. Meeting those demands and tailoring our actions to contribute to the benefit of others are some of the highest ethical demands. Things make sense against the framework of the ethical sphere, and it encourages or more strongly demands that one take others into regard.[61]

If the aesthetic life encourages pursuit of pleasures that are primarily self-directed, the ethical life stresses the importance of duties and responsibilities to others. In many ways it may seem as though the individual subsumes herself to the values of the whole. Our individuality is a matter of how well we meet the demands society puts upon us. While there may be pleasure in meeting one's obligations and expectations, pleasure is not the motivating force. Rather, a desire to fit in makes people want to be proper and upstanding. The social norms that shape us may be very comfortable and give us a stable and secure self-identity. Whereas the aesthete would find this life dull and confining, the ethical man finds this to be the best world. His comfort zone is constrained by the norms and values he holds most closely. The ethical man is sober in the sense of being serious and not frivolous. The most ethical man is the one who acts in accordance with the highest duties and principles. The only time it is acceptable not to meet one's duties or obligations is when not doing so would result in some bigger benefit to the universal.

But this safety and security may well become stifling. What happens when we have doubts about certain core moral values or begin to experience a lack of ease with expectations that others place on us or—perhaps just as important—that we have placed on ourselves? What if we realize we are spiritually anemic? It may provoke an existential crisis that can be profoundly life altering.

Many addicts experience this crisis as some point. Those who remain high functioning may be most susceptible to this sort of crisis. A person may begin to feel as if he doesn't quite belong in his own life. He may be doing everything in his personal and professional life that a good responsible person does. He is a good son and brother. He is making progress in his career and is being an engaged father. He can be an active community member, always one of the first to pitch in. On many accounts, he has it all.

Why might he nevertheless feel a lack of ease about his life, and maybe even that his life is not his own? His life is so full of obligations, expectations, and shoulds. Everything in his worldview or his ethical existential stage says that he *should* be happy, grateful, and satisfied. To be otherwise would be silly, ridiculous, or improper. While meeting all these demands had made him happy before, he may start to realize he is (highly) functioning on autopilot. The great hazard is that a person can lose himself quietly over time. While he may take note of losing other things, he might not even notice he has lost himself.[62] He's in crisis. He's in despair. And he may not even know it.

Despair is a consequence of an imbalance within a person's self. If he is too concerned with his own pleasures, he is selfish in some basic ways. He's all about himself. The ethical man who is so concerned with being dutiful, fitting in, and being everything to everyone else is just as out of balance as the aesthete. He's all about everyone else and not enough about himself. One of the most provocative claims Kierkegaard makes in *The Sickness Unto Death* is that happiness is the greatest hiding place for despair.[63] The ethical man provides a good example. For Kierkegaard, despair is not an emotional or psychological state. Rather, it is a spiritual crisis that can be chronic. To be in despair is to be unaware of, or not suitably attentive to, one's spiritual life. The man in despair is one who does not stand in the right relationship to himself as a spiritual being and therefore does not stand in the right relationship to God. The more the man tries to deny this about himself, the greater his despair.[64]

Despair, as alluded to before, may be a necessary step to faith, which is Kierkegaard's final and highest existential stage. Being in despair is radically disorienting; all bets are off. Despair is an unstable state because a person's regular frameworks for making sense and meaning are failing. Despair is an existential concussion with intolerable symptoms. One cannot reason oneself out of despair. Instead one has to suspend one's reason and leap. There's perhaps nothing more terrifying.

Chapter Eighteen

LEAPING OUT OF DESPAIR

ONE WAY TO LOSE YOURSELF AND EXPERIENCE GREAT DESPAIR IS not to be suitably attentive to *what* you are. Kierkegaard claims that humans are spiritual beings and a human self is an amalgamation of finitude/infinitude and necessity/possibility.[65] Despair results when any one side of these opposites is out of balance in a person. There can be either too little or too much of any one of these, with the following four possible imbalances:

1. To be prone to the fantastic is to allow one's imagination to govern. A person takes flights of fancy so that she isn't grounded. She lacks finitude.[66]

2. To be narrow-minded and parochial is to keep a person from considering how she could be different. How others think of her and how she is seen by others are what govern her. In some sense, she is a generic person and not a unique self. She lacks infinitude.[67]

3. To continually try different things but never settle on even a few for any length of time is to invest one's energies primarily or entirely into possibilities of how one *could* be. This type of self tends to drift away because there is little to anchor her in terms of commitments and priorities. She lacks necessity.[68]

4. To act as if everything a person does is already set or inevitable is to embody a type of determinism. To be ruled by necessity is to assume that things will always be *this* way, so there is no reason to try other things. She lacks possibility.[69]

A despairing person is out of sync with her spiritual nature. All humans are vulnerable to despair. Addicts may experience any and all of these forms of despair; it may even feel like "despair roulette." Careening between forms of despair will produce an existential concussion in fairly short order.

What's the way out of despair, according to Kierkegaard? What might be helpful for people who struggle with addiction and recovery, and anyone who wants a life of genuine (as opposed to despair-hiding) happiness and flourishing? Remember that Kierkegaard was a Christian, so God and one's relation to God play the pivotal role. For Kierkegaard, one must come to understand oneself as a spiritual being in relation to God. In other words, when one's self attends to its relation to itself, other selves, and most importantly to God, one can genuinely flourish.[70] When one stands in the right relation to God, despair is overcome because a healthy balance between all the elements of a self is achieved. But how is one to achieve this balance?

The first step is resignation. Resignation is necessary for overcoming despair and making oneself capable of making a leap of faith. Resignation is the rejection or sacrifice of meaning that is found in the finite world. It is acceptance that having it all in the finite world isn't enough to get you to the infinite or eternal. There's a gap between the two that cannot be bridged by anything made or found in this material world.[71]

Faith is what can bridge the gap but it requires a leap that takes someone from everything he knows by his reason to that which is beyond his reason. Faith requires that we not just acknowledge but embrace that there are things beyond our comprehension, things that are paradoxical. Faith may require a kind of action to which every fiber in his rational being screams, "That's impossible!" Kierkegaard offers Abraham of the Hebrew Bible as an example meant to demonstrate this in its potential horror.[72] Is Abraham the father of faith or a potential murderer?

For those who are not familiar with it, here is the story: God commands Abraham to sacrifice his son, Isaac, even though God had said that Isaac would be the father of nations. Abraham was prepared to do this and at the last moment, God allowed Abraham to sacrifice an animal instead. Kierkegaard offers different ways of understanding Abraham's actions in order to demonstrate that a leap of faith involves a suspension of some or all of the ethical demands one holds dear. It is not easy to have genuine faith; it may be downright horrifying.

Consider Abraham's situation: he is a parent and a devout servant of God. Among the highest ethical obligations are our duties to our children. Parents are expected not only to safeguard their children in the most minimal sense but also to cherish them and treat them lovingly. A parent's obligation to her child is given huge weight in just about any context. We condemn parents who abuse their children; we recoil in horror. We make judgments about who is fit to be a parent. The issue of fitness has to do with how well people will meet the needs and desires of their children. If someone meets all the material needs of a child but is emotionally disengaged from a child, most people would say that something deeply important is missing.

So, here is Abraham ready to sacrifice his son on an altar with a knife. Killing one's son is an abomination; it is a violent violation of a parental duty. Abraham is willing to violate a nearly supreme ethical commandment for his God. There seems to be no larger benefit to others if Abraham sacrifices Isaac. Abraham's sacrifice is different from that of the Greek king, Agamemnon, who sacrificed his daughter to the gods so that the Greek armies could sail to Troy to wage war.[73] Agamemnon sacrificed his daughter to a higher end (though his wife Clytemnestra disagreed and killed him when he returned from the Trojan War). No doubt Agamemnon suffered greatly, but his action could still make sense to him and to others, even as they disagree with it. Agamemnon's sacrifice was for a greater good.[74] Abraham's sacrifice is different. There is no higher ethical end or obligation that the sacrificing of his son would serve.

Abraham's faith in God requires that he embrace a paradox and live a horrific contradiction. He accepts that he will lose his son; this is resignation. He also believes at the same time that he will keep his son. It is not possible for both of these to be true. Abraham accepts this, yet is prepared to act in the belief that by sacrificing Isaac he will keep him. As Kierkegaard tries to explain, God is infinite possibility. With God, all things are possible, even and especially, the impossible. To have faith is to leap into a space or relationship with God where things are possible and impossible at the same time.

Faith is the belief that everything you know and understand to be impossible is possible. It is an unending exchange of "It's impossible. And it's possible. But it's impossible . . . " Faith isn't an act done once a week from the pews of a church. It is a way of being in the world that is embodied and lived every day. Faith requires repetition. With faith a person is able to relate directly to God at all moments; her spiritual self isn't smothered by any of the forms of despair.

If you share a similar conception of God, Kierkegaard offers a great deal of hope. For as much as Kierkegaard diagnoses the anxiety, dread, and despair that an individual may suffer, he also points to the greatest possible joy and happiness one can have. But even if you don't accept this, or any, conception of God, Kierkegaard still has much to offer. One crucial insight is that a person cannot make a successful leap when she hedges her bets by keeping one foot in her old life. The same is true with recovery, as William James noted with keeping some drugs around "just in case." They become an anchor.[75] It is much harder to leap with an anchor around your foot. Another insight is that leading a life of faith doesn't make someone stand out from the crowd in any obvious way. Knights of Faith or Knights of Infinity, as Kierkegaard calls them, aren't illuminated. Knights of Faith outwardly look like everyone else, perhaps the local shopkeeper. Kierkegaard notes that

> most people live completely absorbed in world joys and sorrows; they are benchwarmers who do not take part in the dance. The Knights of Infinity are ballet dancers and have elevation . . . to be able to come down in such a way that instantaneously one seems to stand and walk, to change the leap into life into walking, absolutely to express the sublime in the pedestrian—only that knight can do it, and this is the one and only marvel.[76]

The Knight of Faith/Infinity actively moves through his own life; he doesn't watch his life unfold passively from the bench. And he doesn't just move through life—he dances. In lieu of Kierkegaard's shopkeeper, I offer a person with good recovery. His is an ordinary life in many ways, full of small pleasures, inconveniences, difficulties, and joys. In leading this life of good recovery, he gets back part of the aesthetic life as well as the ethical. There is great pleasure and fun; boredom is not an option. Life feels vibrant and lush, and the person in recovery is able to experience, savor, and appreciate those pleasures. Those pleasures are not shrouded in a chemical haze or hangover; he is able to appreciate them for what they are and keep them rightsized. He can recognize and cherish them only because he has good recovery.

The recovering person is able to recognize the ethical/ universal and meet his obligations and duties to others without losing himself in the process. The person with good recovery is no saint; he's far from perfect and recognizes this. But he accepts this knowing that perfection is a standard that cannot be met.

If the Christian notion of God doesn't resonate with you, you might find more friendly companions in Friedrich Nietzsche and William James. Nietzsche boldly proclaims, "God is dead."[77] God may be dead, but each of us is alive and can make his or her own life meaningful and valuable. James offers a conception of "higher and friendly power" that can encompass a Christian notion of God, but also principles, commitments, and a sense that there is more to the world than just a single person.[78] Kierkegaard, James, and Nietzsche all share a belief that one must make and live a passionate commitment in order to lead a meaningful, happy, and rewarding life.

Chapter Nineteen

WOULD YOU CHOOSE THE
SAME LIFE FOR ETERNITY?

WE'VE ALL ASKED OURSELVES WHETHER THERE IS SOMETHING WE WOULD do over if we had the chance. Sometimes the question is prompted by a disappointment. At other times, we ask it when something we did had radically different consequences from what we expected. Such consequences are usually negative and painful. Rarely do we ask this question when something has gone well. We often ask, "Would I do it again?" when we want to justify a choice we made. If the answer is yes, then we comfort ourselves that we made the right decision. If no, then we probably feel regret.

The "Would I do it again?" question usually has a limited scope; it attaches to a particular situation or set of circumstances. This is a good question for us to ask. We could all benefit from more critical self-reflection about our motivations, actions, and the consequences of our actions. It is also a good way to keep a check on our regrets. Without too much effort, a regret can turn into a very nasty resentment.

But what if you asked that question about your entire life? Would you live your whole life again? And what if you raised the stakes by living your *same* life over and over again for eternity? How you answer this question reveals a great deal not only about the quality of your life but also about the degree to which you take responsibility for it. Are you willing to take responsibility for eternity?

Nietzsche gives us just that challenge. He challenges each of us to completely grab hold and take ownership of our lives. Too many people are afraid to do so; it requires bravery. Nietzsche would say that it is a matter of survival. Too many of us are content to "just go along with things" because it seems easier in a way. For many people, trading away responsibility for their lives is easier than taking responsibility for them. This would make Nietzsche shudder.

Nietzsche was never one to shy away from provocative claims and questions expressed in the most evocative way. His images can be arresting. He wrote

> What, if some day or night a demon were to steal after you into your loneliest loneliness and say to you: "This life as you now live it and have lived it, you will have to live once more and innumerable times more; and there will be nothing new in it, but every pain and every joy and every thought and sigh and everything unutterably small or great in your life will have to return to you, all in the same succession and sequence—even this spider and this moonlight between the trees, and even this moment and I myself. The eternal hourglass of existence is turned upside down again and again,

and you with it, speck of dust!" Would you not throw yourself down and gnash your teeth and curse the demon who spoke thus? . . . Or how well disposed would you have to become to yourself and to life *to crave nothing more fervently* than this ultimate eternal confirmation and seal?[79]

To be clear: Nietzsche is asking whether you are willing to live the exact same life, down to the tiniest detail, for eternity. The kicker is that one needs to make this choice each time one's life is lived. That demon will come into your life at the same point every time, when you are in your darkest hour, and ask that question. There's no wiggle room in answering; it is impossible to hedge one's bets in any way.

This question, "if you had to do it all—exactly the same—again would you be horrified or would you gladly embrace it?" is one many addicts consider at some point in their lives. It is a litmus test of how one understands the meaning of one's life and the responsibility for it. A person might unsurprisingly object, "I've suffered greatly. I've caused huge suffering to others. Why would I choose to relive even some of the moments again? All the bad moments along with the good, even once? For eternity?! Heck no!" Of all philosophers, Nietzsche recognizes that much of life is suffering. His concerns, though, are how and what sense a person makes of her suffering. Suffering doesn't define or distinguish us from others. The meaning we make of the suffering is what defines and distinguishes us.

Meaningless suffering is intolerable; it is the most debilitating existential concussion. We do have the capacity to make meaning of our suffering in ways that can be transformative and life affirming, though most people will not have the will or courage to do this. The unwillingness or the fear to transform one's life is a tragic failure. The attitude of those who "just go along" and are not proactive in their own lives is what Nietzsche derisively calls the "herd mentality." People who are sheep (or "sheeple" as I called them one day in class) would rather stick with what is known—even if uncomfortable and profoundly disappointing—than take a risk.

Nietzsche delivers a stinging critique of Christianity in many of his works, especially in *The Genealogy of Morality*. His argument is that Christianity elevates certain virtues and values that encourage and reward people for being tamed and domesticated animals. People say, "No," to this life in the hopes of getting a gigantic "Yes," to a life of eternal redemption and salvation. For Nietzsche, people who view everything through a lens of "God's plan for us" never take responsibility for their own lives. Such people are willing to tolerate great pain and loss, for example, because of the belief that everything will be all right in some future, perhaps not of this life. People won't be willing to stand up for themselves when they are persecuted, hurt, wronged, or exploited here and now, if they believe they ought always to turn the other cheek and that, in doing so, the first shall be last and the last shall be first.[80]

In many ways, Kierkegaard and Nietzsche differ from each other significantly. But they share one important similarity. Kierkegaard claims each person must stand in an unmediated one-to-one relationship with God. This is just what Abraham was prepared to do. He wasn't a docile sheep because he was ready to sacrifice his son like a sheep. In comparison, Nietzsche is calling on each of us to stand in an unmediated one-on-one relationship to himself. If we let our self-relationship be mediated by Christian values and virtues that reward docility and passivity, we fail to take responsibility for our own lives.

Who are the sort of people who would answer yes to Nietzsche's question and "crave nothing more fervently?" They are the people who are committed to deep critical reflection about their character. They are the ones who would be willing to grapple with Socrates to tend their person. These are people who do not shy away from past actions and take responsibility for who they are and how they show up in the world. They are the ones who will embrace their lives and not run from the difficulties, pains, and suffering they both endured and caused. People who embody and act from will to power are the ones to say yes to this question because they are already saying yes to this life right here and right now. People with will to power do not deny themselves in the hopes of a future reward. These are people who own their lives. Who else could own them? Too many people, Nietzsche claims, give ownership to and responsibility for their lives over to religions and gods.

Some people will take Pascal's Wager and believe and act as if there is a God offering eternal salvation. But others, in a Nietzschean spirit, will reject the wager. They will ask themselves and other specks of dust if they are willing to live the same life for eternity. All of this takes courage for us specks of dust. Who is up to this challenge? Many specks, I believe, some of whom are people with good long-term recovery.

To have good recovery is to have taken the opportunity to transform the meaning of suffering one has caused oneself and others. It is also to make meaning of the suffering that is beyond one's control. Good recovery puts questions of character and responsibility in the center of life; one's self is the most important project of life. This project is life affirming. This is why the person who says, "Yes!" embraces this project and all that came before it, not just for this one life but for all of eternity.

Albert Camus (1913–1960) provides an interesting example of a character from Greek mythology who embraces his life for eternity. In *The Myth of Sisyphus*, he offers an interpretation of Sisyphus who had been condemned by the Greek gods to an eternity of futile labor. In Greek mythology, there are conflicting stories about how and why Sisyphus came to so offend the gods that they sent him to Tartarus, the worst part of the Underworld. Regardless of the offenses, Sisyphus's punishment was to roll a large boulder to the top of a mountain and have it roll back down to the bottom where he would need to begin again. The moments of interest to Camus are when Sisyphus returns to the bottom of the mountain. At the bottom facing the rock again, "One always finds one's burdens again. . . . This universe henceforth without a master seems to him neither sterile nor futile. . . . The struggle itself toward the heights is enough to fill a man's heart. One must imagine Sisyphus happy."[81]

Sisyphus is stronger than the rock because he knows exactly the situation in which he exists for eternity. He recognizes and accepts his reality; there is no self-deception or self-delusion. Were he to wish reality were different from how it actually is, he would be in complete torment. Ruing his fate and blaming others would be a victory for the gods. And for the rock. No, Camus claims, Sisyphus owns his actions and his fate; he is responsible for his condition. Sisyphus doesn't merely acknowledge this though. Rather, he embraces it each time he puts his shoulder to that rock and starts to push it back up the mountain. Sisyphus makes a passionate commitment to himself.

Sisyphus says yes to Nietzsche's question. He lives that answer with happiness each day for eternity. But is Sisyphus a model for recovery? He certainly can be for some, especially for those who don't believe there are external causes or forces that create meaning, value, and even, or especially, redemption or salvation. Nietzsche and Camus together challenge us not merely to accept our histories and responsibility for them but to embrace them. When we do this, we can create life-affirming meaning in the bleakest and darkest conditions. We live the answer, "Yes!" to Nietzsche's question.

Chapter Twenty

IS THERE LIGHT AT THE END OF SUFFERING?

"How much more can I take?"

This question has been at the root of the human experience for as long as we have records of it, and surely longer. It was the lament of Job[82]—or at least one of them—and is asked with no less frequency today, in response to circumstances ranging from loss and grief to the typical hardships of a trying job or a long winter.

But where is that point at which a person actually "breaks" or comes to believe her life is devoid of value or meaning, and that the world is, too? The truth is most people don't really want to ascertain just how much more they can suffer. A vast majority of people would look askance at someone who sincerely wanted to experiment with her own limits for suffering. But what if we were to treat it as a genuine question? Many active addicts confront that limit every day, in ways people who are fortunate to be free of addiction may never know. For some of them, the process of reaching that limit becomes an opportunity to effect radical transformation in their lives.

A broader understanding of this concept is offered by William James. In his famous work, *The Varieties of Religious Experience*, he provides significant insight about the limits of misery and its transformative potential. *Varieties* is the product of lectures James delivered at the University of Edinburgh in 1901 and 1902. His focus is the experiences of individuals "for whom religion exists not as a dull habit, but as an acute fever."[83] By "religion" James does not mean religious institutions and their long entrenched theological debates, but something more akin to an individual spiritual state, which may or may not include belief in a God.

James was uniquely suited to deliver these lectures. He was a physician, philosopher, and a psychologist before the field of psychology was part of academia, and someone with a deep, abiding interest in psychic events. He was, in every sense, a student of human nature. He explored this question of what we may call the "misery threshold" because he wanted to know if some people were more capable or more prone to experiencing "the acute fever" of religious belief.[84] His answer: it is those who suffer most who are inclined to experience that fever. These are the people who fascinated him— those who toed right up to and sometimes over the line of despair and meaninglessness.

James claims in *Varieties* that there are two kinds of people, differentiated based on where they live in relation to their misery threshold.[85] Each person, he argues, has a threshold for emotional pain akin to a threshold for physical pain. While some people run to painkillers at the slightest physical discomfort, others are able to tolerate excruciating physical pain. The same holds for misery.

James calls those who live on the sunnier side of their misery threshold "healthy-minded." Optimism fills their lives, though there are degrees of optimism. Some of the healthy-minded see the glass half full, while others see it as half full with something really delicious. These are the kind of people who always look for the bright side and have a soul with "a sky-blue tint, whose affinities are rather with the flowers and birds and all enchanting innocencies than with dark human passions."[86] Though the sunny-side people can be miserable at times, they have a low tolerance for misery. It would take something catastrophic for them to stay on the dark side of their misery lines.

The sunny-siders are somewhat interesting to James, if only because they constitute a type that is almost completely foreign to him. James knew himself and many of his family members to belong to the second category—"sick souls" and "divided selves," who live on the dark side of their misery threshold. Sick souls tend to say no to life, according to James, and are governed by fear.[87] Sick souls tend to become anxious and melancholic, with apprehension that spreads opportunistically.

The person with a divided self suffers from what James calls "world sickness."[88] This sickness is progressive and James charts its development keenly and compassionately. Those with a divided self experience a war within; they careen through life wanting incompatible things and leave damage in their wake. It isn't surprising that people with world sickness veer between apologizing for past mistakes and committing new ones.

Perhaps not coincidentally, this is an accurate description of addiction. James knew a great deal about drunkenness or "inebriety," to use the language of his time. For years, his brother Robertson (Bob) was in and out of asylums for the inebriate and spent his final years with James and his wife. This may explain why some of the most compelling first person accounts in James's work of divided selves and sick souls who were later transformed come from people who were drunkards. (It may also explain why Bill Wilson, one of the founders of Alcoholics Anonymous, was so taken with William James. He was able to see himself in these stories and, as a consequence, make sense of his own conversion experience when he sobered up for good in 1934.)

James's description tracks our knowledge of addiction accordingly. The first stage of world sickness is "pleasure diminished." What had previously brought joy or pleasure now brings it less often and to lesser degrees. For an addict, the buzz just isn't as much fun. It just isn't the same, yet she will continue to seek it.

"Pleasure destroyed" is the second stage. More and more things are seen as or end in disappointment; pessimism becomes the most frequent response. The pessimism grows, though at this point it still attaches to particular situations in life rather than to the whole of life. An addict may take any disappointment as a reason to use. As more things become disappointing, the more she will understand herself to have reasons to use. Disappointments and reasons multiply in unison.

The final stage is best described as "pathological melancholy." The progression in this final stage is significant. First, a person is no longer able to recognize joy and happiness. She experiences a melancholy and dreariness about life that makes her incapable of generating any joy for herself. The next phase is a melancholy in which a person generates an acute anguish about herself and the world—she feels self-loathing and acute anxiety. Her entire being, James would say, is choked with these feelings. Quite significantly, not only does she see herself as having no meaning or significance, but nothing in the world has meaning. This melancholy leads to utter hopelessness about the particular conditions in which one lives, and the meaning of life in general. With this hopelessness, the drama of repentance and the effort to repair will end. It would take too much energy and it just isn't worth it. Nothing is worth anything.

A person in the grips of the worst melancholy experiences a frightening anxiety about the universe and everything in it. At this point, panic and fright completely govern her. The world is worse than any conceivable nightmare. James describes a man who admitted that a "horrible fear of my own existence," came upon him one night. The man suddenly remembered an epileptic patient he had seen in an asylum who had greenish skin and sat "like some sort of Egyptian cat or Peruvian mummy, moving nothing but his black eyes and looking absolutely nonhuman. This image and my fear entered a combination with each other. *That shape am I*, I felt potentially. . . . I awoke morning after morning with a horrible dread at the pit of my stomach, and with a sense of the insecurity of life that I never knew before, and that I have never felt since."[89] In a letter to a friend after the publication of *Varieties*, James admitted this was his very own experience as a young man. He himself had walked right up to the edge of a yawning abyss.[90] James scholars debate the exact date of this crisis, but most locate it around the time James was in his late twenties.

Nietzsche recognized that "when you gaze long into an abyss the abyss also gazes into you,"[91] while Kierkegaard noted that some people are more afraid of jumping into that abyss than falling. James understood this fear, and saw in it the potential for transformation, renunciation, and surrender of the self. Surrendering the self involves two movements: The first is giving up the incompleteness or wrongness of one's actions or, even more broadly, one's ways of living. You renounce your old ways of acting. The second movement is giving oneself over to the ideals one wants to embody. You embrace new ways of living. When we surrender in this double sense, we may experience "the acute fever" of a spiritual life.[92]

The terms "surrender" and "higher power" and "powerlessness" are apt to leave some people uneasy (they are key phrases in twelve-step programs everywhere). To surrender, in more Jamesian terms, is to make oneself open to new possibilities. To surrender is to stop clutching core beliefs or parts of one's identity so tightly. When a person loosens her grip, she makes it possible to hold something new—perhaps very tentatively—in her hands. In the case of a person whose self-worth or humanity has been decimated, it is a matter of being open to the possibility that just *maybe* she is worthy of a little dignity and respect. Surrendering can be simultaneously liberating and terrifying.

The when, where, and how of surrender depends on a person's misery threshold. Someone with a low threshold cannot suffer long and so is willing to make changes. Others will be able to suffer enormously and not surrender until there is nothing left to lose. Each person's "rock bottom" is the point where she can no longer tolerate the misery.

"Higher power" may leave even more people uneasy. James, however, uses the term in an elastic way. He does admit that "we Christians" call this higher power "God." But to illustrate what he calls a "higher and friendly power," James uses Henry David Thoreau's description of walking in the gentle mist at Walden Pond. Thoreau wrote, "Every little pine-needle expanded and swelled with sympathy and befriended me."[93] Higher power can be nature, moral principles, patriotism, or a sense of fellowship or good will to others. For some, higher power is an "enthusiasm for humanity." Each of these, James might say, takes a person outside or beyond herself and connects her to others and thus can be a higher power.[94]

It's easy to identify how "the acute fever" burned in the Christian saints who engaged in all sorts of acts of self-mortification. It is less easily spotted in someone who has surrendered to and embraced a higher power about their addictive behaviors; there is no equivalent of a sackcloth. There is, however, a unification of a previously divided self. People who know addicts in recovery often see this before the addict does. A person with the acute fever of recovery comes to have a firmness of mind and character. She has clear beliefs and principles, and acts from them. She also has a stability achieved and maintained by keeping various relationships with relatives and friends congruent with personal history, commitments, goals, and beliefs. Each of these helps to hold the others steady. Finally, a person who burns with the acute fever of recovery has equilibrium. She is able to strike the balance between opposing forces, some of which are in her control while others are not.

No one person is immune from all suffering. However, the acute fever can transform a person's life so that the drama, chaos, and despair become, as James says, "severed like cobwebs, broken like bubbles."[95] And this, James would proclaim, shows that hope and redemption are just as much a part of the human condition.

CONCLUSION

Since its inception, philosophy has been concerned with the human condition—what humans are, how we relate to each other and to the broader world around us, and how we make sense of ourselves. Addiction is a particular form of suffering that is part of the human condition, making philosophy especially well suited to engage questions about addiction. Philosophy can offer diagnoses of emblematic features of addiction as well as recommendations or prescriptions for transforming the meaning of suffering that characterizes addiction.

The Socratic urge to clarify the important concepts and realities that guide our lives, and to tend to the well-being of our soul or self, offers much to people struggling with addiction. For some of us, addiction is a concept; for many of us, it is a reality. Answering the question, "What is addiction?" involves challenging dominant views on it. Addiction can neither be reduced to a brain being hijacked nor to a person exercising insufficient willpower. By dismissing these overly simplistic if common perceptions, we create room for more expansive explanations of addiction as a form of suffering in which a person loses himself. As addiction progresses, the mild discomfort becomes intolerable suffering. Suffering is intolerable when it has no meaning and makes no sense. A person may become incomprehensible to himself and to those around him. He can become separated from the people, places, and things that have always helped to ground and define him. Such a separation causes a radical disorientation, which is a regular companion to addiction's suffering. A radically disoriented person will likely suffer from an existential concussion.

Self-deception is another emblematic feature of addiction. Self-deception is an accelerant; it fuels addiction and suffering. It comes in many guises: understanding yourself to be terminally unique; engaging in rationalization and denial, aided and abetted by bad logic; second-guessing and therefore undermining yourself; turning every want into something you must do; holding yourself to unrealistic and unreasonable expectations; engaging in doublethink; and moving from moral apathy to indifference, are all forms of self-deception. They can overlap and crisscross, making a thick weave that is hard to cut through. People struggling with addiction experience any or all of these; each functions to keep a person from clearly seeing and taking responsibility for her behaviors. In other words, self-deception hinders self-knowledge, which in turn means that genuine care of one's soul or self is nearly impossible. One cannot live the happiest and best possible life when one is self-deceived.

Self-deception is much more difficult to maintain in the presence of others; they help us to see ourselves, and the world, more clearly. Some of the help comes from friends and others who know us in our various walks of life. Other times, the help comes from stories of strangers, when we see ourselves in their experiences. Instead of seeing ourselves as terminally unique, we realize we share bits and pieces with others—like the features shared in a large extended family. We see a family resemblance to other people also struggling with addiction or living a life of recovery. As we begin to make a new or different sense of our experiences and ourselves, we cultivate the possibility of a transformation that may be lifesaving and life-affirming.

When active in our addictions, our using is the axis around which most if not all parts of our lives turn. Some of us dedicated our lives to pleasures and passions. Others to following every rule and meeting every expectation others placed on us and that we placed on ourselves. In both of these ways of life, a person can become subject to great despair if he is fundamentally out of balance with himself. Such imbalance means a person has lost himself. One way out of that despair is to take a leap of faith into a new way of living that restores balance. Any leap of faith, but especially the leap into recovery from a life of addiction, is simultaneously horrifying and hopeful. But it is the way to regain the self that was lost.

No one can make the leap for another; it is something that each person must do for himself. Relatedly, no one can take responsibility for another's choices and way of living. Each person is responsible for the quality of his own life. A person who accepts full responsibility for his life would be willing to live the same life for eternity. It is a passionate commitment to certain ways of living. Taking responsibility for one's life is crucial for caring for one's soul or self. This is what people in recovery do.

There is light at the end of suffering. In making a new meaning of one's addiction, overcoming self-deception, making friends, and taking responsibility, we can be transformed and regenerated. We become people who are capable of flourishing and leading our best possible lives. For as much as suffering is part of the human condition, so, too, is joy.

NOTES

1   Kierkegaard, *The Sickness Unto Death*, 32–33.

2   Wittgenstein, *Tractatus Logico-Philosophicus*, 88.

3   Locke, *An Essay Concerning Human Understanding*, 193–201.

4   Wittgenstein, *Culture and Value*, 16e.

5   Monk, *Ludwig Wittgenstein: The Duty of Genius*.

6   Kierkegaard, *The Sickness Unto Death*, 25.

7   Locke, *An Essay Concerning Human Understanding*, 14.

8   Plato, *Republic*, 186–92.

9   Shakespeare, *Hamlet*, in *Hamlet: An Authoritative Text, Intellectual Backgrounds, Extracts from the Sources, Essays in Criticism*, 45.

10   Dickens, *A Tale of Two Cities*, 454.

11   Boss, *Ambiguous Loss: Learning to Live with Unresolved Grief*.

12   Lake, "Comfort Food."

13   Baumeister and Tierney, *Willpower: Rediscovering the Greatest Human Strength.*

14   American Psychiatric Association, *Diagnostic and Statistical Manual of Mental Disorders.*

15   Nietzsche, *Will to Power.*

16   Wittgenstein, *Philosophical Investigations*, §268.

17   Flanagan, "What Is It Like to Be an Addict?," 289.

18   The expression "form of life" appears in §19, §23, and §241 in Wittgenstein, *Philosophical Investigations.*

19   Ibid., p. 174 and §415.

20   Wittgenstein, *Philosophical Investigations*, §67.

21   Descartes, *Meditations on First Philosophy*, 23.

22   Kierkegaard, *The Sickness Unto Death*, 93–94.

23   Descartes, *Meditations on First Philosophy*, 26.

24   Wittgenstein, *Zettel*, 41e.

25   Aristotle, *Nicomachean Ethics*, 102–4.

26   Pascal, *Pensées.*

27   Aristotle, *Nicomachean Ethics*, 25.

28   Cohen and Bonifield, "California's Dark Legacy of Forced Sterilizations."

29   *Stuart Saves His Family*, directed by Harold Ramis (1995; Hollywood, CA: Paramount Pictures, 1995), VHS.

30   Kant, *Grounding for the Metaphysics of Morals*, 25.

31   Ibid., 26.

32   Ibid., 26.

33   Ibid., 30.

34   Ibid., 30.

35   Ibid., 36.

36   Ibid., 38–39.

37   Orwell, *1984*, 36.

38   James, *The Varieties of Religious Experience*, 282.

39   Kant, *Grounding for the Metaphysics of Morals*, 36.

40   Ibid., 32.

41   Ibid., 31.

42   Wiesel, Interview with Alvin P. Sanoff, "One Must Not Forget," 68.

43   Hume, *A Treatise of Human Nature*, 416.

44   Aristotle, *Nicomachean Ethics*, 141–43.

45   Ibid., 110.

46   Aristotle, *Nicomachean Ethics*, 18–19.

47   Hume, *A Treatise of Human Nature*, 415.

48   Hume, *An Enquiry Concerning the Principles of Morals*, 18–20.

49   Ibid., 51–61.

50   Ibid., 18–20.

51   Ibid., 61–68.

52   Ibid., 68–72.

53   *Alcoholics Anonymous*, 59.

54   Descartes, *Meditations on First Philosophy*, 17.

55   Descartes, *Discourse on Method*, 12.

56   Aristotle, *Nichomachean Ethics*, 119.

57   Ibid., 121–24.

58   James, *The Varieties of Religious Experience*, 152.

59   Wittgenstein, *Culture and Value*, 64e.

60   Kierkegaard, *Either/Or*.

61   Kierkegaard, *Either/Or*.

62   Kierkegaard, *The Sickness Unto Death*, 32–33.

63   Ibid., 25.

64   Ibid., 15–17.

65   Kierkegaard, *The Sickness Unto Death*, 13.

66   Ibid., 30.

67   Ibid., 33.

68   Ibid., 35.

69   Ibid., 37–38.

70   Ibid., 15.

71   Kierkegaard, *Fear and Trembling/Repetition*, 46.

72   *Holy Bible with the Apocryphal/Deuterocanonical Books*, 17–18.

73   Homer, *The Odyssey*.

74   Kierkegaard, *Fear and Trembling/Repetition*, 57–58, 79.

75   James, *The Varieties of Religious Experience*, 282.

76   Kierkegaard, *Fear and Trembling/Repetition*, 92

77   Nietzsche, *The Gay Science*, 167.

78   James, *The Varieties of Religious Experience*, 242.

79   Nietzsche, *The Gay Science*, 234.

80   Nietzsche, *On the Genealogy of Morality*, 16–23.

81   Camus, *The Myth of Sisyphus: And Other Essays*, 123.

82   *Holy Bible with the Apocryphal/Deuterocanonical Books*, 447–48.

83   James, *The Varieties of Religious Experience*, 19.

84   Ibid., 125.

85   Ibid., Lectures IV and V, "The Religion of Healthy Mindedness," 78–118.

86   Ibid., 80.

87   Ibid., Lectures VI and VII, "The Sick Soul" and Lecture VIII, "The Divided Self and Process of Its Unification," 119–170.

88   Ibid., 128.

89   Ibid., 147.

90   Letter to Frank Abauzit, June 1904. Quoted in William James, *The Varieties of Religious Experience*, 508.

91   Nietzsche, *Beyond Good and Evil*, 279.

92   James, *The Varieties of Religious Experience*, 187.

93   Quoted in James, *The Varieties of Religious Experience*, 242. See Henry David Thoreau, *Walden*, 125.

94   Ibid., 242 and 183 footnote.

95   Ibid., 235.

BIBLIOGRAPHY

Alcoholics Anonymous. New York City: Alcoholics Anonymous
World Services, Inc., 2001.

American Psychiatric Association. *Diagnostic and Statistical
Manual of Mental Disorders 5.* Washington, DC: American
Psychiatric Association, 2013.

Aristotle. *Nicomachean Ethics.* Translated by Terrence Irwin.
Indianapolis, IN: Hackett Publishing Co., Inc., 1999.

Baumeister, Roy F. and John Tierney. *Willpower: Rediscovering
the Greatest Human Strength.* New York: Penguin Group,
2011.

Boss, Pauline. *Ambiguous Loss: Learning to Live with Unresolved
Grief.* Cambridge, MA: Harvard University Press, 2000.

Camus, Albert. *The Myth of Sisyphus and Other Essays.* Translated
by Justin O'Brien. New York: Vintage International, 1991.

Cohen, Elizabeth and John Bonifield. "California's Dark Legacy of Forced Sterilizations." *CNN*, March 15, 2012, accessed March 5, 2015, http://www.cnn.com/2012/03/15/health/california-forced-sterilizations

Descartes, René. *Discourse on Method*. Translated by Donald A. Cress. Indianapolis, IN: Hackett Publishing Co., Inc., 1984.

————. *Meditations on First Philosophy*. Translated by Donald A. Cress. Indianapolis, IN: Hackett Publishing Co., Inc., 1993.

Dickens, Charles. *A Tale of Two Cities*. London: James Nisbet & Co. Ltd., 1902.

Flanagan, Owen. "What Is It Like to Be an Addict?" in *Addiction and Responsibility*, Edited by Jeffrey Graham and George Poland. Cambridge, MA: The MIT Press, 2011.

Holy Bible with the Apocryphal/Deuterocanonical Books. New Revised Standard Version. New York: American Bible Society, 1989.

Homer. *The Odyssey*. Trans. W. H. D. Rouse. New York: New American Library, 1999.

Hume, David. *An Enquiry Concerning the Principles of Morals*. Indianapolis, IN: Hackett Publishing Co., Inc., 1983.

————. *A Treatise of Human Nature*. Oxford: Oxford University Press, 1989.

James, William. *The Varieties of Religious Experience*. Cambridge, MA: Harvard University Press, 1985.

————. *The Varieties of Religious Experience.* New York: Barnes and Noble Books, 2004.

Kant, Immanuel. *Grounding for the Metaphysics of Morals.* Translated by James W. Ellington. Indianapolis, IN: Hackett Publishing Co., Inc., 1993.

Kierkegaard, Søren. *Either/Or Vol. I.* Translated by David F. Swenson and Lillian Marvin Swenson. Edited by Howard A. Johnson. Princeton, NJ: Princeton University Press, 1971.

————. *Either/Or Vol. II.* Translated by David F. Swenson and Lillian Marvin Swenson. Edited by Howard A. Johnson. Princeton, NJ: Princeton University Press, 1972.

————. *Fear and Trembling/Repetition.* Translated by Howard V. Hong and Edna H. Hong. Princeton, NJ: Princeton University Press, 1983.

————. *The Sickness Unto Death.* Translated by Howard V. Hong and Edna H. Hong. Princeton, NJ: Princeton University Press, 1983.

Lake, Larry M. "Comfort Food." *Slate,* November 8, 2013, accessed March 5, 2015, http://www.slate.com/articles/life/family/2013/11/families_dealing_with_mental_illness_need_support_too.html.

Locke, John. *An Essay Concerning Human Understanding.* New York: Dover, 1959.

Monk, Ray. *Ludwig Wittgenstein: The Duty of Genius.* New York: Penguin Books, 1991.

Nietzsche, Friedrich. *The Will to Power.* Translated by Walter Kaufmann. New York: Random House, 1967.

———. *On the Genealogy of Morality.* Translated by Maudemarie Clark and Alan J. Swensen. Indianapolis, IN: Hackett Publishing Co., Inc., 1998.

———. *Beyond Good and Evil.* Translated by Walter Kaufmann. In *Basic Writings of Nietzsche.* New York: Modern Library, 2000.

———. *The Gay Science.* Translated by Walter Kaufmann. New York: Random House, 1974.

Orwell, George. *1984.* New York: Plume, 2003.

Pascal, Blaise. *Pensées.* Translated by W. F. Trotter. London: Dent, 1910.

Plato. *Republic.* Translated by G. M. A. Grube, ed. C. D. C. Reeve. Indianapolis, IN: Hackett Publishing Co., Inc., 1992.

Shakespeare, William. *Hamlet.* In *Hamlet: An Authoritative Text, Intellectual Backgrounds, Extracts from the Sources, Essays in Criticism.* Edited by Cyrus Hoy. New York: W. W. Norton & Company, Inc., 1992.

Stuart Saves His Family. VHS. Directed by Harold Ramis. Hollywood, CA: Paramount Pictures, 1995.

Thoreau, Henry David. *Walden.* Boston, MA: Beacon Press, 1997.

Wiesel, Elie. Interview with Alvin P. Sanoff. "One Must Not Forget." *U.S. News & World Report*, October 27, 1986.

Wittgenstein, Ludwig. *Philosophical Investigations*, 3rd ed.
Translated by G. E. M Anscombe. New York: Macmillan,
1968.

———. *On Certainty*. Edited by G. E. M. Anscombe and G.H.
von Wright. Translated by Denis Paul and G. E. M.
Anscombe. New York: Harper and Row, 1969.

———. *Zettel*. Translated by G. E. M. Anscombe. Edited by
G. E. M. Anscombe and G. H. von Wright. California:
University of California Press, 1970.

———. *Culture and Value*. Translated by Peter Winch. Edited
by G. H. von Wright. Chicago, IL: The University of
Chicago Press, 1984.

———. *Tractatus Logico-Philosophicus*. Translated by D. F. Pears
and B. F. McGuinness. New York: Routledge, 2001.